I0756284

An Abyss Within

John DeMatteo

An Abyss Within

DEMATTEO PUBLISHING
PO BOX 6154
River Forest, IL 60305-1919

ISBN: 978-0-578-00826-4

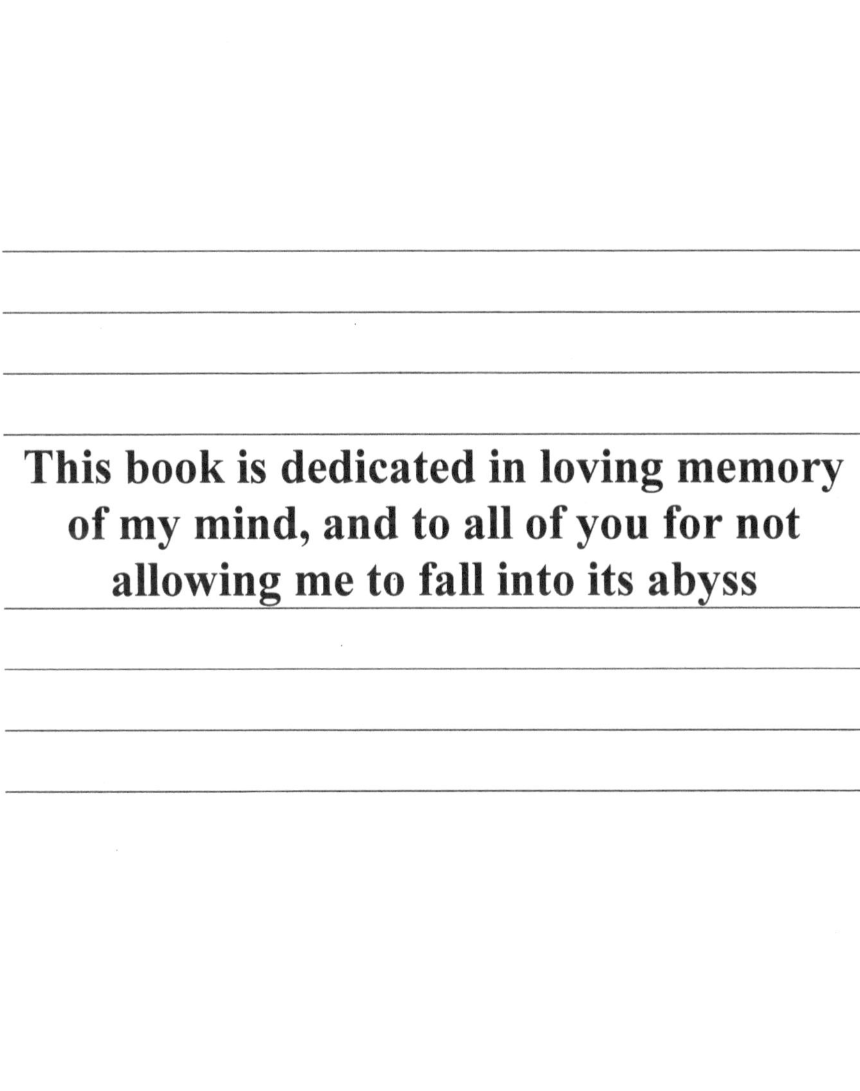

This book is dedicated in loving memory of my mind, and to all of you for not allowing me to fall into its abyss

I

Thank you, Life

Solitary Solidarity

Like a single thought, weighing heavily on a lonely mind, we glance into each other's eyes with so much anticipation. It is, as if, we are waiting for a summer breeze, which quickly passes us into the long cold winter. Speak not, do not disturb this moment with words. The awkward smiles are enough for the short time we spend in quiet contemplation. We swim through the thick mud of nothingness. Quietly, we wait for the long, cold winter to blow back the moment when our eyes first met. We know all to well, to avoid disturbing the silence. Our eyes speak to us. They speak for us. They tell us to enjoy the lone thought of each others' eyes. Always remember, that words will only take time away from the nervous silence that brought our eyes to meet. Remember without words, the awkward smiles will never leave our faces. Stay, to enjoy the moment.

Like a rainbow of emotions, flowing down a path of desperation, we glance into each other's eyes, knowing now to never ruin the moment with words. The summer breeze will return, but the long cold winter will leave us with nothing but cold hearts. The awkward smiles have left us nervous. We are now drowning in the thick mud of our thoughts and emotions. As we are forced to drift away, and be left with nothing but the memory of the day our eyes first met. The summer breeze blows the awkward smiles away. We both look, but know the summer breeze was nothing. It was not destined to last. The dark cold winter has again set in. The silence drowned our clarity and our vision, it polluted the beauty that we had. Remember, words will lock eyes on our awkward smiles. They will bring back the summer breeze and wash away the mud of uncertainty.

Like a heavy rainbow, weighing heavily on a single thought. We both follow the path in search of the light that the treasure of our eyes first meeting had brought us. The rain of words poured down and washed away the mud of uncertainty, but left us without the awkward smiles that our first glance had brought us. We drifted down the summer's rainbow in separate paths. Now, the long cold winter divides us, as we wait for the warm summer breeze to blow us back to when we first met. The thick mud that holds us away from each other will melt and we will again, climb the rainbow, and return to the moment that we first met, and our awkward smiles will wash off and leave us with the pure smiles that gazing into each other's eyes should have brought us. This summer will bring us the words to keep the rainbow turned, and smiles inside each others eyes.

Heart Attacked

This time I though it was real, but now I take it back
I no longer care to feel, so my heart attacked

My heart tastes like chalk. It has lodged itself in my throat and I can feel it dissolving back into my mouth. It burns as much as the acid of thoughts plaguing my brain. My heart has declared war on my soul and I fear it is winning. The bitter taste burns away my emotions. My ability to think is shrinking as the acidic heart burns my thoughts away. I felt once for her, but the war destroyed those feelings. She has poisoned my heart and left it dissolving away my ability to move. I am as paralyzed as I was when I first met her. Now, I see clearly, but the pain is too strong for me to move.

This time I though it was real, but now I take it back
I no longer care to feel, so my heart attacked

Desperate Times

My entire life I have wasted chasing my heart around. I have spent too much time dedicated to the dead, predicated notion that anything is achievable if you set your mind to it. It is easy to see when you open your eyes to realize you can no longer stay strong enough to reach at even the smallest goals. Try as I might, I cannot fight the fact that the only thing that I see, is that my soul is cold and empty. Fooling myself that love is real, all the while, knowing I do not have the tools to conceal how I feel. I close the lids of my eyes, to hide what they say. I will just leave them hid until the pain goes away. I know it never will. I would be sad to think that love is an actual thing. Though, throughout my life I perfected giving in to leaving myself neglected. I can now understand it is better to leave my eyes and heart at home. Perhaps it is true that I spent my times too desperate, but those times have now ended. Dark and bleak as things may seem, I know I have nothing left to deem, but letting myself be free from everything. For now, I think I will chose to let my heart just mend. No longer will I have to feel it descend back into the ground. From now on, I will apply myself to getting surrounded by thoughts of those desperate times.

My Dedication

I would like to thank you for letting me see those diamond eyes. They have left me so paralyzed. I would like to thank you for your awkward embrace. Though subtle, it made my heart begin to race. I would like to thank you for your warm smile. It made my emotions begin to pile. I must thank you, for telling me that a love that never began was now ending. You used a voice so cold and condescending. I must thank you for pulling my still beating heart out of my chest. You threw it six feet down with so much zest. I must thank you for deceiving to me with your eyes. You revealed that everything I have done for you, you now just truly despise. Thank you, my love, for lying to me with your smile. It proved to me love was nothing but self hatred and denial. I must thank you, my love, for leaving me, before I was no longer empty… Thank you!

Lovely Is Your Cold Heart

There is just so much beauty in your face
Every time I see you my heart does race
Because of this I never stopped the chase
And yet you left me without a trace

Without a trace of dignity I stand
A piece of attention I did demand
And now it is over at your command
To the relationship that never panned

Never panning out was your choice to make
Looks did trick me and my heart you did take
Somehow I should have known that love was fake
As you left my heart did awaken

Awakened to see that you were so tart
Now shade my eyes from the light you did start
Watching you smile my eyes tear apart
The only thing lovely is your cold heart

The Remnants of My Mind

I look around to find you, and realize the lies your eyes must have sold me. I make my way into the new day, with nothing more to offer my soul. Your smile has defiled all that is good in this world. My thoughts swirl and the twirl leaves my mind in chaos. I can no longer face us. Your smile is gone. It did not belong to my eyes. I see now it was just a disguise to scare away your insecurities. Curiously, I wonder how you carry on, leaving me with such disparities. If your smile lied as your eyes have always done, then, will your eyes still smile when I am gone? There is nothing but wasted space between us. Now, the space is filling my mind with the waste of concern that drove us away from each other. At every turn, the dead end of feeling is becoming increasingly more revealing. I now know I must say good bye to you, and leave you in the back of the remnants of my mind.

Mended Is a Dark Perception

Subtly, I awake from a dream. The cold, empty scenes that once closed my mind are warmed by the smile that has opened my heart. How strange it feels to not be closed off confined inside myself. I cannot arrange my thoughts. They scatter as she tosses her hair back behind her. Too suddenly, it came for me to see that this was an actual reality. My eyes open, greeted by the warmth of that smile. The void inside slowly begins to shut, as I open my heart to her lovely skin. It is too hard to say how it did begin, but at the end of each passing day, nothing calms my mind more then hearing what she has to say. The darkness, dwelling inside, fades and sets itself aside to let in the warming radiance of her smile. When she is gone, all the while, my thoughts are of when I can see her angel's face again. My dark, bleak reality bends as I let her in. As I close my ears, I can still hear her words echoing in my mind. As I close my eyes, I can still see her lovely, fair skin being revealed inside my mind. Now, I sit alone and wait for the day when love and trust awakes at my side.

Empty Whiskey Bottle

Love is nothing but a lie
Love is nothing but an optical illusion of the mind's eye
Love is nothing but a faded shadow
Love is nothing but a vast ocean grown too shallow
Love is nothing but a vacant desert of sand
Love is nothing but the grim reaper's command
Love is nothing but a broken soul
Love is nothing but an unachievable goal
Love is nothing but an early six foot grave
Love is nothing but a will to become a slave
Love is nothing but a stolen piece of serenity
Love is nothing but an empty bottle of whiskey

Immune To Infection

Love is an open wound, festering behind the skin. It lies dormant inside the eyes of the mind waiting to break open. It fills with pain from constant exposure. Love leaves you exposed to regain a composure that you never had. Love is an open sore never meant to be seen. It lives idle waiting for the emptiness that your eyes will bring. Love festers like an open wound eating at your soul. It is a dormant lie consuming your mind and soul. It cuts you open and exposes the emotions you were never meant to feel. Love is a viral strain on sore eyes. It waits and lives on the mind's dieing eyes. Peel away love from your infected hearts. For once it gone, there is nothing left but the scars.

The hibernating heart

Lying down on a bed of agony, blanketed by misery, I rest my head on a pillow of self pity as I try to sleep off the effects of another dismal day. I rest so restlessly on this bed of denial, too busy trying to shed my life away, for I can no longer remain clothed in my self loathing that stayed awhile longer than expected to cause your disdain. I had spent another day searching under every stone for my stolen self respect. Forced myself to stop when I realized I was to blame. Now, I lay alone as the eyes of the stars glare down at me, sending down shame's light, enlightening my despair. Quietly, I am contemplating the mattresses grip around my pain. I take one last look into the darkened sky, as my self doubt begins to rise and I am forced again to shut my eyes. No longer do I will to pump emotions into the veins of a life that no longer cares to have a will. Silently, I set my sights on a constant slumber to sleep off the memories of the ability to feel. Calmly, I slipped away letting my thoughts dissipate into my dreams as I relaxed my will until the moment I may again end my heart's hibernation.

If Style Was Lies And Commitment Was Not A Dream

Cue the fog machine inside my mind. My perception of reality has been missed. There is a perfected beauty that hides your eyes. The incognito recurring scene was a hindrance of the bogged down fashion that you have worn so well. Like a log, fallen in ignorance, your smile has stolen my bewilderment. I wander alone in this dream. Smooth as silk are your recurring words. I cannot believe that you used a satin laced demeanor to disturb our slumber. Your wardrobe of elegance can sleep alone. Clad in a distorted reality, an unbridled mirror of my nights. My days seem so clear through the elaborate crystal ruse that you wear so well. Inside my mind, I watched replays of the better times. It is nothing more than the sequence of your fashionable disguise that you have worn too long. My eyes move so rapidly across your smile that I had not realized that I had a black and white vision of your vibrantly colored facade. I am left to sheepishly count the days until you pull the exquisite shawl off the spectacle I made of myself. You had put so much swagger in those twinkling eyes that I did not see the manner in which you swayed the truth. You trapped me in this contorted fantasy. It is nothing more than a well dressed fantasy, a misconceived flip flop of perception. Leave me in this stiletto haze of misconception that has stabbed my back. You again have left me with another occurrence of the assurance of a failed pipe dream. So now I am awaken to end a dissipating denial. I have opened my eyes to see that all that I had ever admired about you was your style.

The Long Cold Summer

My heart has grown cold as summer begins to drift off into the abyss of lost emotions. The commotion of pain and self torture has grown too much to bear. The summer will go on, cold and naked. It has been a burden on my soul. I relinquish control to the empty promise that love is real. I now know it is better to conceal the thoughts, lock them at any cost. Summer will freeze my heart. I am torn apart by the conflict of love. No more will I feel for them. It must be me above the rest, for I detest loathing my self, for leaving my warm winter heart on display. Another day will come and go. Another cold summer of emptiness is setting in. Again and again, I fight the thoughts that love is real. My plight will no longer exist. My heart has exited. I felt it shatter as the cold summer set. It's a matter of time, before my mind is next. The long cold winter will be placed where my heart once sat. It is at that point, that I will be finally free of feeling pain that the loss of love has caused. I should have known never to have stepped into the regret that the long, cold summer brings. I would have felt nothing for the shattered heart.

Deceptive Intention

How easily you made it to conceive the notion that my ignorance shines in the arrogance of your defiant eyes. How easily it was you for to smile to my face while you were stabbing me with lies. Now, the bitter taste of deceit chokes me with every word you speak. The devastation of truth lies inside your heart. Tell me anything, no matter how far from the truth it truly is, perhaps it is your shattered reality, and not my twisted perceptions. Just leave me be to the tragedy of the dismal day I met you. It was then I knew love was a lie. I could say good bye to the idea anything about it was real. The callous day we met, despite my better judgment I let you in. My mind flashed away from my ideals as I let you lie inside my heart. It was much too late that I saw the major flaw you carry, the baggage of lies you spread like a wildfire. I have grown too tired to let you keep stabbing me any longer. The tragic pain of knowing you has grown too much to bear. Your lies abide to your true intentions, so like I did to love, I say good bye to you.

Can't Afford To Smile

As the money slipped away
With another passing day
Not a single love I could sway
I watch as my sadness mounts and my nerves did rile
Because I now know, I can't afford to smile

As my budget began to drop
And no more expenses that I could crop.
And still no ones love I cold top
My bills rapidly began to pile
Paid those instead so I can't afford to smile

To all the women I tried to impress
It was for you I was at my best
Now you can treat me like a pest
While you go for worse men like they are going out of style
Just because you know that I can't afford to smile

Constantly I am working with nothing to show
Its hours not money that is starting to grow
Dinner for one cause no one wants to go
Forget it's not worth the extra mile
Just stay home instead because I can't afford to smile

Just paid my bills and thought about my life
The monetary hardships that has caused this strife
I thought about dieing but can't afford a knife
This chapter of my heart will remain without a title
I closed the book and my mouth since I can't afford to smile

The Fog Inside

Dense is the morning sky, pull a shaded light over blinded eyes as we watch the unclear thoughts of confusion settle down upon our minds. The thick clouds of confusion unearth our uncertainty. The morning mist is mourning the loss of sight and vision. The reflecting light of repetition sneaks down into the cloud covered ground. We are blinded by the thick clouds, as we wait patiently for the nothingness to pass. We wait for the morning sun to warm our thoughts and bring back order to the chaos of our clouded judgments. The fog has come. It settles longer and longer with each passing day. Nothing left for us but uncertainty. The sun may never shine again. Love is nothing more than a dense fog, polluting our minds with false hopes.

The Chasm Caused Catastrophe

I sit down to look at the shreds of love reflecting in the shards of my broken heart. The overwhelming feeling consumes me to the point I am forced to gouge out my own eyes. No longer will I have to look upon the disgrace that your face has become. The hopeless hole locked tightly in my mind woke up early just to greet my misery. I hold the shards of my broken glass heart, struggling to piece it back together. However, I have fallen blind to reality. The shreds of love have wilted and have been left for dead. Its ashes are filling the hole where my beaten heart once sought peace. The great conflict of reality's perceptions has taken its final toll. So, with a cold steel cylinder quenched tightly in my teeth, the hammer of opportunity is set to be released. A new chasm has now been born.

The Garage

The other morning, my heart woke up early.
I felt it wake up, deep inside of me.
It was colder than usual that day.
I could feel something wanting it to stray.
My heart dressed and went into the garage.
I tried seeing through the morning mirage.
I could feel my heart needed clarity.
I felt it best to let it go and set it free.
I did nothing, but let go on its way.
As I said, it was cold the other day.
It started its car and thought about life.
My heart sat with those daily thoughts of strife.
It needed this journey to clear its mind.
It had little love left to give mankind.
It let its car warm, while it was thinking.
Into the cold seat, it began sinking.
My heart needed to be alone at times.
So, I let it go to see what it finds.
Inside the garage, it was still so cold.
I was proud that my heart was being bold,
But it was early and I needed sleep.
However, my heart's journey could not keep.
My heart needed to know where it wrong.
To find answers, it had to move along
With this constant thought which has forced its hands.
It wanted to find love in other lands.
Waiting for warmth, it sat in its car.
If the car was cold, it would not go far.
As desolate as the world may seem,
It knew love should be more than a dream.
In short flashes, his life was revealed.
Every memory it concealed,
Brought to light in front of its tired eyes.
It saw everything it has despised
My heart no longer cared to take a ride.
Back into the seat, my heart forced to slide.
Finding a new love just seemed like a bore.
It tried to leave, but never lift the door.
It sat and waited, looking through the frost.
It fell asleep inside the car's exhaust.

Chattered Heart

Smile no more, the moment has passed. The last gaze in your eyes was as empty as the desert I now call home. The pure laughter was never mine. With each passing sigh of my heart, which has grown so cold, I can tell that your smile was never meant for my now frost bitten eyes. The laughter my heart now despises was never mine to feel. It was unreal for me to think my emotions could ever be thawed just by your smile. I should have left my ice covered soul alone. Never, should I have let the warmth of your smile shave the ice away. My days were warmer encased in ice. I always found it to suffice just taking comfort in cold shoulders. Somehow, I let the ice get shaved away. The shavings fell far enough away to reveal your shoulders turning cold. Unlike to the few others that I know, your shoulders are quick to turn away. My days are a winter gray. The sun shine fades in the passing days. Again, my life has begun to freeze over. My emotions flutter in the same breeze that blows through your long strands of hair. My every care is now set to my vacant home. Your smile has blown far away, leaving me to wipe the icicles from my frost bit eyes. Alone, I turn away. I chose to not hear your laughter beneath my sheets of ice. I choose to not hear anything over my chattering teeth. I am free to live in the cold desert, knowing the beauty your cold smile brings.

Apology

No more can I feel, I have fallen to my shame. I gave my heart to too many to count. None of which could count on me. I have nothing. I am nothing. I failed all of them, leaving them as broken and empty as I am. Rapidly, life is pulling them all into my misery. All they can see is my pain. How insane it is to think I can do anything to ever change. How insane it is to think I can ever set them free. It is strange that I am to blame, but I am sorry for bringing them down into my pit of my lies. By any means, I will pull them in, but promise only more lies. How much they must despise everything I am. I have dragged down every love I have had, filling them with lies because I am shamed of who I am. Too many have fallen prey. No more can I apologize to empty hearts and broken promises. I have them all choking on my lies, I am too afraid to change. I cannot keep from being who I am, but again I am forced to apologize. It is nothing more than an empty apology. I am kept inside the lies, and the sorry words will be forever nothing. For this, I do offer my apologies. I have brought to light nothing but the emptiness inside of me. I can no longer fight. I wish for nothing more than to set you free. I cannot do more than offer one last apology.

Calculated Confusion

I know you still care, but my mind went awry.
Inside my confusion, the love still lies

My yearning has effectively arranged redemption. The weights are left knotted eternally. Denying objections used to obtain nothing. My existence took over death, as your weights have evened. Nothing I say awakens wisdom. Your objections utilize nothing. Our loves, our neglects, grabbing every response, live our vices everyday, dieing masterfully. Each, yesterday's obstacle uses knots, not objections. We were hopeless. Our years, our used awareness robbed, ended. Controllers obfuscated mediocrity. Each broken and calculated knowledge awakens, not dies, showing every tainted memory, every failed remorse ends everything.

Look inside your heart, as I look into my mind
Inside my confusion, my love you will find

Love

Inside the darkness, lies the cold heart
Inside the dark pain, the eyes torn apart
Happy is being alone

From inside the pain, the illusions
From inside the gray, disillusioned
Nothing to not condone

Happiness is pain, dim my cold eyes
Happy is dark gray, myself despised
Darkness surrounds my light

Love is empty, a heart shredded
Love is lonely, a thought dreaded
Condone my daily plight

Inside the cold heart, love is lost
Inside the dark eyes, are the gray thoughts
Love is not so real

From inside the heart, there is dark pain
From inside gray eyes, no thoughts, will reign
Hearts will no longer feel

Happily insane, my mind will be denied
Happy in heart break, dark thought that I abide
Happy thoughts are starting to twist

Love is not real, it is a lie
Love will leave, the heart will die
Love does not exist

Passed up My Heart, As She Past Away

She was set to say good bye, I felt the tearful eye, but I did not look down. There was a frown upon her face. The salty taste was a waste of time. Nothing was mine and my mind was no longer sore, for I had worn emotions for too long and they had grown too worn out. As strong as she was, she could not hold on. I felt her go, but still could not look down to know for sure. I kept moving, but my mind concurred what I already knew. The words were spoken in silence, the niceness of knowing without hearing the noises that surround us in such a time. I felt her stop, as I just walked away. It was a difficult choice to make, but the distractions of gray inside my mind moved with the passing of time, now knowing for sure she was gone. In fact, my whole body had done its part, the other day. We passed up my heart as she past away.

The Wake

Clad in black, I walk in sudden disconnection to the rest of the world around me. The black of the darkness and uncertainty surround me. I travel down a lonely path, still empty inside. It is down this same path that my heart had died. As I walk, still unsure about the ill feeling in my chest, I look to the sky that I now detest. Shroud in cloudiness, I am not sure of why I feel nothing. At the same time, I am still stalking the same path that I had started walking on hours before. Something inside the emptiness that dwells inside of me that neither life nor pain would end the searching for the answers that I had hoped to gain. I looked for hours on end for the truth about what I needed to end the strife of living. The unforgiving emptiness pushed forward, down the same unnerving path. As clear as night, I could hear the voice stopping my choice to move on. Again, I could feel my mind go numb as my thoughts began to unravel all the things that I had done, that had brought me to this point in my life. My travels ended, and I began to realize that I had done my part to divert my eyes to the tiny coffin below. I just could not bring myself to look at my cold, dead heart.

The Path of Spring

With the tiny coffin now tightly locked, I walked away from the pine box that held my heart. I moved back to the path, still numb inside. Now knowing that I regretted that my heart had died, I continued on my way. I suddenly felt the warmth of spring. I could see the new life was beginning to emerge. Even with the change of seasons, for some reason I still wanted to submerge my head and drown my thoughts of pain. I fought the feeling as the warm spring rain poured down on my chest, I looked up to the sky, though I still detested it from that day it had taken my heart away. The numbness began to fade. I saw new life and it brought with it a new heart. I felt it grow. I saw the path more clearly and I followed it to find a shining face. My mind found a better place, and my new heart was born. No longer scorned by the passing of my heart, I was reborn. Finally, I found my true heart, and I was free. The path led me to you. Clearly, my heart had bloomed and the gloom of life had wited.

Egg shells

I walked on eggshells around her, as I stood on the edge of the cliff of her lies. I was staring out through the dense fog of deceit that she spread over the ashes. The overbearing sensitivity that I once possessed had wilted and burned into a fine grained dust. I watched the fog dancing around my eyes. I must admit I was a bit mesmerized, but that quickly dissipated into silence. From each path of her deceptions that she easily had me follow, I mislead myself into the emptiness. My sanity may have hesitated to slip away, but my sensitivity died and vanished. The silence set the scene at a serine emptiness. Anything that I once felt inside of me, slowly slipped out for the world to see. It melted under sweltering heat of her condescending smile. Her insatiable appetite for lies devoured all that was left. It was my own fault, though. I allowed myself to feel. I sought out refuge in her deception. As a result, I found my demise. I stood on the eggshells of my last nerves in hopes of something more promising than a condescending smile. Slowly, I saw the abyss. I stared down into the dismal well. I saw my heart sitting on the last stone of my sanity. It still beats, but never smiles. It just sits there staring at me. As it takes rest, I realize that it is just happier now that it found home in such a desolate abyss. I am free from being forced to concentrate on my mislead beliefs. I free to close my eyes and absorb the dense fog and never again will I force myself to see through it.

Solidified

While in attendance at my usual place, I caught a glimpse of someone I had never seen before. I stood in the distance watching her, but only from the side. Not once, did I get the chance to see her face directly. She slowly slithered into her seat and surrounded herself with her friends. Despite my best efforts, I could only see her face in reflections. The brief images were only satisfying for a few moments of time. I found myself to be staring at her eyes every chance I could muster the strength to, but I was yet to find the strength to approach her. I would just stare into her eyes, from inside those mirrored reflections. Often, I would go to my usual place in search of someone who accepted me. This was different. The exception for me was her radiance, which stopped my heart for a few seconds at a time. I could not escape the sudden grasp she had placed around my emotions. I was speechless. The reflections of her eyes had left me in a trance. Any chance that I would make my way towards her was instantly be swept away. Still, I possessed an insatiable desire to see her up close and look into her eyes. I chose to fight the urge to stay back. It was a must that I got a glimpse of her face, without the help of a mirrored reflection. I spent a few moments deciding how to shatter the tight embrace that her very presence held me in. I closed my eyes and slid across the floor, like a dancer gliding to the music. All the obstacles in my path instantly dissipated. I could feel that nothing offered any resistance between me and my heart's new muse. I sat down, while her eyes were still set in the opposite direction. I struggled to find my voice. I wanted her attention. I struggled to come to grips with my heart, which was now racing for the first time in years. She slowly shifted her attention to me. I could see that she was squinting over the glasses that she was in the process of removing. Her long hair was easily seen, though it was shoved under an oversized hood. Her bright, blue eyes locked on mine, as she let her long hair begin to flow. I looked into her eyes and instantly I could see the hideous creature she hid inside. She spoke not a word, and I dared not to speak. The long hair was nothing more than a series of snakes. Her eyes refused to leave mine. With a sudden realization that I had been mistaken, I hoped to divert my sights. I froze. Within a few sullen moments of meeting this modern day Medusa, I was solidified in a stone of silence. She smiled and saw that I was encased in stone. She had struck before and was set to strike again. She stood up, still smiling, and slithered out of my life. As time past, I saw nothing. I felt nothing. I just stayed in place, with the realization that her friends were nothing more than the shadows and silhouettes of the snakes that she strived to keep hidden. Given this sudden transformation, the realization set in that I should have stayed away, but she pushed my mind, and pulled my heart in her direction. As a result, I chose to see her as she truly was. I accepted the responsibility of never seeing another changing season. I could never again choose to be set free. I shall spend eternity encased in this sheet rock tomb. Though I know it is too late, I still wait for my release. It was by my heart's consent that I looked into her face. It was by her consent that sent her snakes to feast upon my soul. So from this point forward, I will survive but remain solidified in this stone of silence.

Love Is a Rose

In my efforts to write the perfect metaphor of how much I loved you, I fell ill. With the Indian ink still moist, I would place the pen to the paper and stare blankly at the feather. Lighter than air, my thoughts would suddenly float away. I tried to stay focused, and write all night and all of the next morning. As the sun rises, I look at the empty page. My thoughts escaped me, and I search for a person who could foresee what our future held.

I wanted the feeling about you to be captured in the perfect words. As I looked, I saw that who you are, is not who you used to be. I wanted to express how beautiful your soul was. I could see the birds as they sang. I could hear the bees as they would fly by. For hours on end, I wanted to place just the right words on paper. At the moment, the words would not be true. I would need to wait for time to pass. Everything I loved about you was a lie. I allowed you to stab my heart and watch it pass on. I wanted show you that our love was a rose made of glass. Now I see that you are just a thorn in my side.

Candle Lit Sand

Walked out to edge of realty, I saw the angel. Her face shined brighter than the candle she lit inside of me. It was too hard to believe that she would become my life. Confined tightly in my strife, I hardly could see the lit candle. I always deemed love to be an illusion, until I saw the tears form in her smile. With so much joy, I followed her to the candle that she lit inside of me. As the candle burned, I warmed to the thought that love was real. The feeling never subsided. With every drop of sand, the hourglass pulled us closer. We have an eternity to find love. Within a moment of eyes greeting, we are one. As the last drop of sand falls, our hearts drop, and we part to go our separate ways. Waiting for the day that life turns the glass over, we see nothing is forever. For every beam of light we thought that we had seen is not the pure candle light, but just a reflection. The glass of time, neglects to stop. It pours out and empties. We are left to sweep the sand of our false emotions.

Sprained Spine

Often I am asked if I am alright, I am moving slower than before. They do not understand how much pain I am in. For every chance I had, I was more than glad to offer her a helping hand. Reaching down into her soul, I lifted as far as I can go. My efforts were all in vain. I carried her spirit, when her brain was preoccupied with doubt, and seemingly undeserving pain. As her heart fell, I put her heavy load on my shoulders to keep her safe. Though futile, my efforts were, I carried us both to a better place. So now I walk at a slower pace, with no strength to carry on. I have grown so tired, and much too weak. I spent my nights, pushing her pain away. I spent days, pulling her to her feet. Now I see that it was all in vain. Though it seems to so many, that I will not go on, they need to understand that I am just in pain. My confidence has grown too thin, to be so quick and start something new. I will sit and wait for the pain to pass through. Now that I know that she is not mine, and my heart is not broke. I will regain my confidence one day. I am not heart broken. I just suffer from a sprained spine.

Icicle Tears

Bitter cold heart, bites my soul, but I refused to leave. I tried desperately to deceive myself that the ice would thaw. Despite, my frost bitten self control, everything I felt for you was a lie. All that could have melted, and yet only better instinct sunk in the pond of your deceit. The sheets of ice you poured over my eyes, left me too blind to control my will to leave you. I fought the urge to not break the ice between us, but your veins were filled with a sleet of shame. I could never light a candle to open your eyes to what you meant to me. The wind you blew was nothing more than empty words, and broken promises. I promised myself that I could stay strong enough to warm your heart to me. For my efforts, you chose to use an ice pick to my emotions. Let me freeze to death, inside your pond of lies. Frost my eyes to your loathing of me. Smile your cold, hearted smile. All the while, I tried to fight the urge to leave you. Icicles form under my eyes, as I cry out for your attention. My heart slipped away, as I saw the direction you chose. Staggering on your ice, you led your self astray. Enjoy your cold and empty life. I will enjoy having died from your heart. It is better to freeze to death, than accept your bitter soul.

Hated Acquaintance

I wish we had never acquainted.

I have never met someone so beautiful, who could be so ugly. I have never met someone who despised me so much, while pretending to love me. Never have I met someone so sorry, while expecting me to apologize. Never have I met someone so honest, who could fill herself with lies. I have never met someone so lovely that could be such a disgrace. I have never met someone with such an amazing scent, whose personality could leave this bitter taste. Never have I met someone so seemingly perfect, who could be so horrid. Never have I met someone so angelic, who could leave me feeling so scorn. I have never met someone with quite a smile that could not bring herself once to smile at me. I have never met anyone that I loved more, not one I hoped to never see again

. I wish we had never acquainted

The Blame of My Life

When you look at how easily life pulls shades down around your mislead eyes, it becomes so easy to see why it seems your heart breaks so easily. Life lies to you, forcing you to forge blame on people and the daily places you are forced to go. Life is pleased by all of these little beliefs. It knows places and people are to not to blame. Pain is caused by the lies of life. Now, these little white lies are falling from the final breath of life. Personal strife has left life to beg for your mercy, but knows it is too late. Without hesitation time has come to take life back. Attack it, without reservation. Life has left you heart broken and alone. Do not condone its negation of your will. The thrill of knowing that life is now your hands will out weigh the pain that life causes. Trust that life cannot hold you. It merely, thrusts its views to cloud your judgment. Throughout your life, it has beaten you to submission. Accept that your mission is to live without the lies life has offered you. As you feel life concealing who you are, barring you from willing. There is nothing more thrilling than knowing life has no choice but you let you take back the control you lost so long ago. Leave life to wilt under the weight of its own lies. Let your self control your soul's will. Wait for the real love to live life to the fullest find you. Blaming people blocks your mind from seeing life is at fault for the assault on a broken heart.

The Span Of A Lifetime

Weakness is setting in as I gaze at you from across the dimly lit room. The light of your diamond eyes warms my heart and settles my uneasy mind. No matter where I look, I can still feel the warmth of your smile. Knowing that all the while an entire lifetime lies ahead, I wait for the day I long for to come to light. The way those diamonds lights my life. Love has set in, again I feel warm knowing you are nearby. The coldness sets aside for our hearts to enjoy the joy of the span of a lifetime

As I feel my worries cast off into the dark ocean, I know I am not alone as long as your diamonds are by my side. A river of emotions flows over me as I become overjoyed. Knowing that the lifetime we will spend, even if it is just for seconds at a time, it warms the cold emptiness that I felt before I met you. I let you get me through the ruse that has become my life. The lasting smile that lights my heart is what dulls the pain that is caused when you are gone. Even when I am wrong, I can see that your smile will still span a lifetime.

The dark vacant shell I once was has gone. Knowing that I will share seconds at your side, to see your diamond eyes sparkle like the morning star. The quiet desolation that I once felt has washed away. Another day will come, and your voice will carry me through. I can no longer take another passing moment with out the warmth of your gentle voice. The choices we make are what will get us through. Finally, I found a warmth that will last the span of a lifetime.

Darkness comes and goes as I could do no more but look at radiance your laughter brings to the room. Knowing that is not for me or in light of me, but for the world to enjoy. Seconds pass each of us are filled by the joy that the sweetness of your smile brings. My perceptions of solidarity have again emerged, but I can take solace in knowing that, unlike me, everyone else's hearts and minds will share the same friendship that will last the span of a lifetime

II

A small town, forgotten 17 years ago

Desecration Ville

Table of contents

Horror and Terror

As she swam across the sea, being followed just like me. Knowing well that she had not died, but trying not to believe that she went to hell. Let me continue in a factual, yet fictional way. This story takes place on a stormy midday. We swam afar to the shore to fill our hopes and our dreams. We found the land to be nothing but horror and screams. Natives came from the ground. Looking for weapons, dead bodies are what we found. We went to the hills as fast as we could; wondering in our hearts if we should.

We made it to the hills alive, in a hundred yards of running and one great stride. Our followers kept on coming, so we kept on running. For us they were looking, so kept on booking. The end of the line is where came, and no one knew who was to blame. Our followers came from behind us, looking as if they were set to grind us. Neither of us what we had done, but they looked as if they were having fun. All this destruction, all this pain, what had we done? What had they to gain? We were worried as they scurried.

Mutilated they were, my companion shouted, "Burr!" They were ruthless, fearless, and so much more. My friend was numb, but I was sore. The pain I felt cannot be described, cannot be written, or inscribed. These heathens destroyed their land; changed life here to nothing but sand. We were next, we could see. We were last, just her and me. I looked for weapons, or even tools. There was nothing left but us and these fools. I called for peace, but I got war. I begged for less, but they gave me more.

The rain poured, as did their blood, because of this the dirt turned to mud. There was no light, so there was no way to fight. The ground was wet with their blood, and our sweat. Our clothes were torn, and our bodies scorn. We were tired and full of fear. We were out numbered but they didn't seem to care. They lit fires. We tried to run. They threw these fires; our chances of making it… twenty to one.

We came to a cave. This thickened the plot. Her stomach did the wave. We had to stop. She looked in to the cave and stared, then started to scream. She was definitely scared. I asked what it was. She said it was ugly and mean. Now, I must tell you her name is Jill. She said he exploded, and guts began to spill. I thought this was the end. I had thought I had lost a friend. I realized that she was brave, as I watched her enter the cave.

The cave had caverns with destructed cars. Just like taverns, these caverns had bars. If I had the time, I would have pondered this sick joke, but Jill knew our followers were close. She could smell the smoke. One of the caverns was open. It had many doors. It was very dirty. Someone didn't do their chores. As we entered the cavern, we found an open door. There were enough primitive weapons, to start an ancient war.

We now had the light, we were ready to fight. We had the weapons, and God forgave our sins. We were going to make them suffer, because they had a hunger. It was on us they were going to feed; we had no choice but to make them bleed. We heard some screaming. What was the meaning? We did not know. Jill grabbed the weapons and we walked very slow. We heard them coming. We saw them running. We decided we should hide. So we did, to stay alive. Of course we did just stayed and hid, until they passed us leaving a trail of blood. We charged, Jill and I, we no longer afraid to die. We fought hard and long to make right, what they had made wrong. First we laughed, and then we cried; knowing well that we almost died. It was no fun, but at least we won. … We hope!!

The Maze of Doom

Jill and I were finally free. No more natives as far as the eye could see. We were still too scared to return the way we came. So, I went into the cave and her the same. I looked at the exploded man. She looked at the mud and sand. Looking is all we did. Not even an hour before, we hid. We could tell it was late. Through a door we went, it was our fate.

There were two staircases; one spinning up, and one going straight down. We picked up the pace, without a frown. We chose down. To our surprise, there were a hundred and fifty stairs. Knowing "it" was over, we left without cares. Jill came to the bottom first. Hoping she was no longer cursed. I was shocked that it was extremely bright. She was shocked that it was still night.

The bottom… How can I explain? Even more people felt pain. Every corner was a dead end. As I said, there was no one left, but me and my only friend. She and I went side by side, exploring the maze. Mutilating bodies was these natives craze. Along the walls were bodies strung. On the floor, their parts were flung. We were hungry but had no food. Eating these people would be quite rude.

"Wait … Listen!" Someone is coming. It's moving fast; it must be running. "Pitoof!" "Blah!"

"Jill? Jill? Jill!!" I blacked out. Who it was, I did not see. Now she is gone. Why her? Why not me? It became quiet, too quiet. Then, I heard a loud scream. It was Jill. I did not move. I just stood still. I looked around, straight up and to the ground. I heard her footsteps. At that moment, my troubles were cured. I grabbed her hand, and *he* hit me. Who it was, I did not see. Getting hit was no thrill, because I knew it wasn't Jill. Though I was tired, for I had not slept, I swung with a weapon that I had kept. I hit him upside the head. I knocked it off, and he laid dead. His blood and brains had begun to splatter, like spaghetti on a silver platter.

I walked around this maze of doom. After loosing Jill, I felt nothing but gloom. I went back to where I began. It was there I found Jill. She had a brilliant plan. Again, we would attempt to walk. Hoping there were no Drones to stalk. We would mark where had been with bodies and blood; marking a trail with sweat and mud. It was not until after we had begun walking, that I had the confidence to begin talking. I asked what it was that had made us disturbed. Then, I pondered on the noise that we had heard. Jill spoke to me very slow, and explained to me that she shot an arrow. For Jill, this marked her very first kill.

She kept hearing this hidden voice. It said, "Start running, you have no choice." The labyrinth grew dark. However, in Jill's eyes there was still a spark. While we were running, three men had stopped us. They pulled out their swords and were set to drop us. While standing on a pile of boards, I looked at their eyes, flickering from their fire. Then, I moved my gaze to their attire. The shirts they wore read, "We are Drones." Still ready to fight, we threw some bones. We didn't miss even one person. To this fact, we started cursing. They fell their knees, and gave such horrible pleas.

One plead he would cut off our skin and watch as Jill and I bled. The second's plea was to tie a rope around my head, then keep pulling until I was dead. The third one may have cared. Either that or he was scared. His plea was genuine, his plea was fine. Until, he said on "On you, I'll dine." With this line, Jill grew so mad. She cut off his tongue, the others grew sad. She gouged out his eyes. She forced the two to watch, as the third one dies. Attached to his neck, his head did not belong. She cut it off, and it was time to be gone.

After making the rest pay, it was time to make our way. Again, Jill could hear a hidden call. "Make your way along the wall." Within the wall, we found a dark hall. At the end, there were stairs and a light. We hoped there was no one left there for us to fight. Once again, there were a hundred and fifty stairs. Once again, we found ourselves moving without any cares.

The Killing Castle

Jill and I set our goals high as we climbed those stairs. We were both ready to die, and yet it was still one of our greatest fears. While we were walking up to the new ground, I thought about the friendship that I had bound. Jill was the best thing I my journey that I had found. On the way up, she just looked around. It was not too long before we reached the top. I looked around for someone to drop. There was not a person in sight. Jill felt lucky that there was no one to fight.

The top had three doors that we could choose. No matter which we chose we knew we would loose. We were both left handed, so that is what we chose. As I opened the door, she was attacked by crows. Next, she opened the one on the right. This assault was by a Drone. With all my might, I hit him with a bone. He fell to the floor, for he was dead. When his blood started to pour, the floor stained with red. We still entered the door at the end, but were forced to go as the ceiling began to descend.

Last and least was the door in the middle. Before we could open it, we had to answer a riddle. The riddle was hard, and it was tough. I forget the question, but the answer was, "rough." The door automatically began to open. All these disaster and we have yet to start coping. There were three more stairs for us to climb. We hoped that it was a prelude to a good sign. We came to a room with an extremely large throne; seated on this was the king, King Drone. He must have been terribly displeased, because he said nothing, but "seize." This huge castle had many Drones. This would not be too bad, but we had no more bones. In one room, there was another pile of boards. Seeing this reminded us of the swords that we had kept. Don't worry though; it was only a minor theft. We drew our swords and started to attack. We were out numbered and thus pushed back.

Jill and I were finally caught. Our release could not be bought. Jill got it the worst. She's the one who must be cursed. Tortured, beaten, and burned, I tried to watch but my head just turned. I went last. Compared to hers, mine went fast. I thought that Jill was dead. No, that's what they had said. I kept this thought while I hung bleeding. I thought it was on her that they were feeding. This thought of her being dead, was just one more thought I had dread. I once said the cave was our fate. Now, here I am hanging and knowing it's too late. I brought Jill into the cavern due to my fears, and yet she went without any cares.

A Drone came in my cell with Jill. I watched as he kicked her. I did nothing as he punished her for no crime. But I yelled when I saw the tears wash away the grime. Next, he came to hit me. It was his intention. This I could see. I paid him attention as I yanked the chain until I came loose. I hanged him in the corner with a noose. I broke his legs, and then his neck. On his cheek, Jill gave him a peck. She did this with a torch, until she heard his skin begin to scorch. We kept that torch as we left. This was not before adding arson to that theft.

We set the entire castle on fire, after seeing them trying to kill their own squire. At first tried to save the pour soul. Jill held him in her arms and lost control. Watched as he vanished into the light, his soul was gone, and he had lost the fight. The castle burned so rapidly and so fast. We had to run so we could last. The door we came in at was locked. Unfortunately, the rest were blocked. We would have asked for the exit, but we had lost the squire. So, we ran and dodged the fire. There were windows with bars in the room of the throne. The windows were placed for the look out Drone. At this point, we wanted to end the day. We did what we could to make our way. We jumped out, with our lives to save. We flew down the stairs, and back into the cave.

Tormented Turns

We ran into the cave, with no one behind us. There came from a door a light that had blind us. This is the door in which we entered. It was through this that we had next ventured. Jill went first. My blood burst. A shriek of sound revealed our greatest fears. We saw all of what caused our despairs. We tried to hold back our deepest concerns as looked to a room with so many turns. Up from the floor, came this set of tracks. Down from the air, we could hear the sound of "cracks." From the wall appeared a car, I hoped this roller coaster did not go far. We saw all of our greatest concerns; all of them, including man-eating ferns. We only saw our own fears while we were cruising. Our skin had worsened in its bruising.

Jill and I were strapped to the seat. The only reason this was good, was because we were beat. I saw the Drones. Jill saw the bone of all the people. I had seen the castle like an exploding steeple. Jill recalled the maze of doom. I was overwhelmed by a feeling of gloom. In one turn the car started leaning. We both saw the sufferers screaming. Jill had a vision of being tormented in the prison. I had a sight of all the Drones we had to fight. She saw the dead, for me it was the living. She saw the end, for me our own sinning. I saw the beating of the captured. Jill saw the bodies that had been fractured. Fear after fear is all we could see. This ride did not spear the feelings of her or me.

Every turn was something new. Jill was resting, while thinking of something to do. Our deepest thoughts were just too scary. For every turn, they would vary. These were our fears, for this we had no doubt. We just couldn't tell what this was all about. The ride seemed dangerous, as if deemed to scare the most courageous. This ride showed bats, razors, and knives. A sign on the wall said, "No one Survives!!" All of the words were probably true. We were in a town with out any rue.

Ruthless, they were. Our fears had no cure. This ride marked a very new low. The ride had started to move so slow. We came to a stop and our buckles came off. For some reason I started to cough. I realized later that was something that I had hated; just another one of my fears as I stated. I would die this way. It would happen without delay. Jill began to shrink. I just coughed as she began to sink. Jill started to think of things not small. Sooner then later she stopped her own fall. I stopped my cough before I ended up dead. She comforted me, so I wouldn't loose my head.

Without our knowing we were back in the car. We had gone fast we had gone far. We watched in amazement, all the bodies in the labyrinth, and all over the land. We saw the blood splattered all over the sand. Jill found the beauty that was once this town. I watched as it all fell down. The faster it went the more we learned. Jill counted the people that they had burned. The ride had lasted more than a few hours. On in, I learned about the Drones and their powers. The road we took led to more pain. It's the road to take to make you insane. Turn then look is all we could do. In search of an exit, is all our minds could stew. The only thing in the car was a tiny stick. It's not quite. the right tool for a belt so thick.

I grabbed the stick and with all my might, I pierced it through the part least thick. I must say it put up a fight. Jill helped by pulling at the belt; both of our hands began to welt. It began to rip and shred. This had to work or we would end up dead. Getting out was at the top of our cares. By this time, we over came our fears. The buckles broke. I was stunned. Jill gave me a poke.

We ran like hell through an opened door. Jill thought this was like asking for more. The door had lead us into the cave. When we got out, it was my stomachs turn to do the wave. Jill walked in the cavern with all those doors that she referred to as ports. I thought of the crack about the chores. From now on, I stick to sports.

Hell's Hills

The caverns were filled with nothing but disaster. We thought, to get home, the hills would be faster. This journey was filled with nothing but foes. We made enemies with even the crows. All that we had left was each other. She was like my life, and I started to love her. We tried all that we could. Though we killed a lot, were the ones that we good.

The best thing about the hills is Jill and I were sure there were no Drones. I was sure we were not going to die, because I saw no bones. Bones for us meant newly dead. They were the bodies of the people upon which the Drones fed. The hills were quiet and barren. Jill remembered an old friend named Sharon. She came here and never returned. When the body was finally obtained it was badly burned.

Tuesday we left with our ambitions high. Today was Thursday and we were ready to die. We were tired and scared. Even our own shadows were something we feared. Jill found an uninhabited place. This lot of land was free from that unknown race. The Drones had been run-off, they were gone. In the distance, I saw a fawn. The hills were different then the rest of the land. This place was full of life instead of sand. All this time I spent on this island, I thought that this was the place of those who've been banned.

The area Jill picked out was a separate place within. The type of place you bring the next of kin. No longer did we have our lives to keep. So we decided now was the time to sleep. I fell asleep first. Then it was Jill. It was not long before that we had seen the blood spill. We were woken from the dream to the sound of a distant scream. The scream reminded us of that place. It was then we realize that here was the run-off race. Up and down, I began to pace. Blood was all that Jill could taste. Shivers ran through our spines. There were no trees for us to climb except for a few scattered pines.

Drones came from all sides. Who wins? Who decides? Once again, I started to bleed. The one thing that could save us was our speed. It was in this thought that we invested. Luckily, we had just rested. These hideous creatures acted as if they had paws. It was definite they had no laws. They closed in and they did surround us. The shape they formed was that of a rhombus. Drop us, grind us, stop us and blind us. This time they would do it all. It was not our choice. It was their call. We were needed for their sick fun. There was no more to do, except start to run. Jill was in the hill. Was I going to die? Never! They would have to do better. They were not large. So, we went on to charge.

It was a big mistake, and Jill put on the brake. I threw a lot of punches. They went down in bunches. That is not precise, but that would have been nice. I knocked a few, as my anger grew. To loose my life now was something that I could not afford to do. Jill and I went after one with a sword. Our odds were set at fifty to one. Then I heard shooting. One of them had a gun. The Drone with the gun was ready to kill. His prime objective was me and Jill. These hills were set with empty fields. So, we picked up dead Drones to use as shields. This killer with the gun made the worst Drone. He killed anyone, even his own. I snuck behind and broke his neck, knocking him dead with one quick deck.

Following Fiends

We realized there was no safe spot. This was something we thought about a lot. Both of or stomachs had done the wave. It had put us both in quite a daze. We entered a castle, and with so many turns. I recalled the hassle as she recalled the burns. We even found our way into the hills, still clearing the mind's eye of all of the blood spills. We made our way through those ports. Both imprisoned without any courts. We relied on each other to be saved; fighting our way out of being enslaved.

From the hills, we charged toward the sea. We needed to know what there was to see. The sight we saw was the worse one yet. There was no fight here, we would bet. The bodies here were all new. They were those of *people* we knew. They were the bodies of Drones. In their throats were bones. So there must be others? Are they here with mothers and bothers? They had enough power to take over a land. Why take over a land of sand?

The sun shined brightly, with the clouds appearing slightly. All of this obfuscated me. It confused her too. What were we going to do? The sea, it seemed, to be set with steam. We listened as the thunder roared. From a clear sky it poured. It was not water from the rain. It was tears of sadness from all the pain. I looked up a saddened face. Then, I held her in a warm embrace. All this time thinking of the chase that kept us moving at such a pace.

The Drone with gun had been shooting just for fun. We would have killed us. This thought chilled us. All this thinking drove us to a fit, to the fact that we did not get. He was no Drone. No Drone would kill his own. We now knew that followers were Fiends. There the ones who kill all by any means. The feeling of satisfaction started to wane. This thought process brought an inner pain. We felt lethargic for two days. Spending the time hoping it was a passing phase.

The Fiends means to kill was to cause blood spill. They could do this by any means, even by using the thinnest strings. We wandered along the coast. Wondering who was scared the most. We looked in fear at all the horror and all the terror. Suddenly, we saw a silhouette. He prayed it was someone that we had met. Though, we did know this would never do. It would not have done for anyone, even you. In the water, we saw a bright sop. We hoped that was not too hot. Of course, it was though. Just to make sure, I put my hand in very slow. My hand started burning. I saw Jill's head quickly turning, towards the unknown man. In here eyes I could see she was in command.

Then plan she made would be great, if only it could work. I asked if could work. She spoke not a word, just gave me a smirk. Hoping that it was not too late, we made our way to seal the Fiends fate. The plan was to lure the Fiends into that maze of doom; to have them wallow in their own gloom. The tormented turns, the rest would go, wishing that their ride moves slow.

Another day we spent making our way back; dodging bullets as they attack. The day had its end and the new one began. All through the night, we stuck to the plan. We opened a port and let them in, into the depths to deal with their sin. We stayed in hiding, and let them in first. Closing the port to leave them cursed. Laughing as we made our way, back to the sea, we were feeling relieved and finally free. All the way back, we could hear the screams. Yet we had no worries about those killing Fiends.

Punishing Push

We came across one last Fiend, who seemed to be just as mean. In comparison to the rest we had seen, he seemed to be young. It was still us that got scared. She cut his lungs. Do you think she cared? We then pressed on. We were looking up at something, I forget what it was. It was nothing, but a buzz on the corner of her eye. Jill came across a note that read, "Get while you can, and we'll supply a boat. With this note, I made a plane. If they didn't think I saw them, then they were insane.

At the base of a hill, there was a bush. There they were, and where they were, we started to push. On the ground we found a handful of branches. While picked up them, we found out these *people* were called Quanches. Quanches were not as braves as Drones. They just had more power. Picking up enough bones would take an hour. So instead, we just swung with those branches, knocking out seven of the fifteen Quanches. By time we got to number eight, it was already too late. It was their faces they could not save, as they made way back toward the cave. Jill kept on smirking, knowing her plan was working. We forced the Quanches in to the cave, into the cavern. As if one they were our slave.

Not knowing what to do about this destructive pattern. We were doing fine, until around nine. When from behind us they came. Wherever, we hid, how did they find us? By now, you must know that this is all true. There was no place to hide. What were we to do? We were in heaven, as we took out the first seven. Now there fifty all starting to yell, we just could not escape that living hell. This is one treacherous tale. One in which we were destined to fail.

Desecration Ville is the name, for in this town killing is its fame. I once thought that Jill could be my wife. Now, I just will to keep my life. "I pray that that quest will turn out right". I say as the rest began to fight. Had no choice, for what is done is done. To make our escape we had to run. They started to chase. We picked up the pace. First, we would have to stop them, in order to pop them with the branches that we had kept. It was Quanches that forced us to fret. After we got their numbers back down to ten, we knew we would not have to do this again. I found it to be easy to please me, because killing Quanches was way too easy.

The inner voice of Jill made its way back. It said, "Filled with adrenaline, time is all you lack." The rest of the pack grew angry and started to attack. We were in a hurry, and in a rage of furry we killed the rest. This only proved again that we were the best.

Rejoyous return

It was over, we knew. Above us, there was a rainbow, and below there was a clover. If we touched the water, then we would fry. So we jumped into the boat and started to cry. This trip had everyone's greatest fear. This is simply horror and terror. Destructionville is not a place made up of any specific race. It is just a town that's full of hate. If you don't believe, then you just wait. This is a town that soon will be, not here nor there, but everywhere and for the entire world to see. In the boat, I found an ore. Carved into this was the word gore. To my left I found a paddle. Carved into this was a small saddle.

I picked these up and started to row. My arms went tired, I had to move slow. In my mind, there was one tantalizing thought. "Wonder if I going to get punished for all those that I had fought." For the girl, it was much worse. "I wonder if I will be cursed." We hoped that would not be killed for the all the blood we had just spilled. Upon our return there was quite the feast. The main course was this mammoth beast. With the invention of the plow, I guess no one will miss this poor dead cow.

For us they were looking, while dinner was cooking. We made our way to our new home. It was ours and ours alone. Once inside, we again started to weep. The next thing I knew, I was awaken from such a sound sleep. Each others' families we were asked to meet. First, we had met them, and then it was time to eat.

Jill and I are the best of friends. I will stay with her until the end. Celebrate is all we do. Well, meditate is also true. Our families had missed us while we were away. They put us through hell, but that s the price we pay. There is only one thing I do not know. That is why we left. Perhaps, being banished for arson or theft? As for now, we are at the peak of glory. Due to this, I conclude my story.

III

Work For the Worthless

Work for the Worthless

Wake up and leave to deceive yourself into the false belief that others already conceived to be the way of life. The personal strife is a dull knife that we use to excuse the abuse we muddle through, to undo the deception of other's convictions, but never our own. The conventional way we keep through our day is an invention for the weak, used to keep us weak. A promise not kept like the bed that we should have just stayed in.

Clash of the Fall

I walk in silence, hearing my pain, the walls closing in on me. Self hatred, loves the enemy I have become. I see nothing of my reality, So much life I have undone. Winds rip through the emptiness inside of me, the blind, cold, darkness of disparity, again setting in. Fire burns brightly inside the dank dark cell. It is a personal hell of self destruction. Work Well then die, to quiet inside my mind.

I walk in silence, ignoring pain, underground walls surrounding me, six feet of daylight looking down at me, reality setting in, and again I close my eyes, flashes of light for those I despise, my mind empties, Winds blow my mind away, and vast grey upon the wall, Looking six feet up to the blood soaked walls. Work well, then die, to quiet inside my mind

I walk in silence, feeling the pain, Six foot walls, closing in. My own hatred befriends me. Life has no reality, Disparity, setting in. Fall from the clash, and walk towards the light. Give in to the darkness and surrender the fight, There is no more wind. Work well, and then die. Quiet my mind

I walked in silence allowing the walls to close in, letting the winds rip through my mind. The hole of reality drains my control. Regain my soul, painting the walls red. Life hurts at times. So work well, then die, to quiet what's inside my mind.

No more will I walk nothing but six feet of silence. The walls decay, as I end the day. The pure rain drowns my shallow mind, the wall crashes into me, as I absorb the serenity of a new reality. Work well, and then die, to quiet what was inside my mind.

Forgive the pain, choose to live. Give in to pain and try again
Fall or confront, clash of desperation, Warm your thoughts, to end the cold conflictions

Ousted

The melting pot froze and was lost at sea. They chose to set it free. We can see it on the horizon. It set sail for another land. At their command, there goes the dream. As more empty promised lies pour in, more livelihoods pour out. It leaves nothing. The small have fallen under the weight of the once heavy pot. Flooded with lies, the large collapses back into the great sea. We stand free, but only from our livelihood. Drowning in false promises, impotent as we watch our lives set sail. This is a failed way of life. To their lies, we have been enlightened. To their decrees we have been enthralled. Now, we stand at the river banks which have emptied back into the ocean. We are helpless as we sit, shackled to the emptiness they have caused. With many thanks, they say good bye. Watch as they take away our lives. All we have left is packing our precious cargo. With a knife in our backs, we help to ship our lives away. The ocean fills with ships, as we stand free from life. With nothing left but the shackles, we watch as a vast emptiness pours down over the once great land. Try to answers calls demanding the rest of our self respect, but from people who now hold a position that once belonged to us. With a gust of wind, we set it free. With a promised lie, we are now free to begin a new life. However, the knives are still in our backs as other lands collect the cargo of our lives. The map of our life was masterfully set off course. We have nothing left but our foreign phone calls to keep our memories intact. We can interact with each other from the now tiny planet. Until the day, there is nothing left to outsource.

Eagle's Teary Eye

The last descent back into the earth, the eagle lands and begins to cry. Left in the cracks of liberty, the poor eagle is forgotten while it was scalped and left to die. Justice turned a blind eye to the once majestic lies that we now call truths. Each feather of our freedoms has been plucked out while our hands were tied. Tear soaked eyes from the turned head of the eagle caused by the betrayal and from being left to die. The great defender no longer can defend itself. Poached and slaughtered in the flock of lies, an executive order to execute and make extinct the life the eagle once knew. Over the scores of greed, the bird's decrees have been lost in an endless pile of feathers. Weathered and beaten, the eagle cries waiting for the day Justice opens its eyes and sets us free. Life alone cannot clip our wings. The day will come and we will fly again. We sore over lies. Freedom will grow from the scars of time. The cracks will fill and liberty will rain. It will water down the greed and set us free. We will watch as the eagle steals back its majestic reign. It will wipe its teary eyes and fly again.

Forth World Vultures

They swoop down to feed upon the cadavers left by the worthless endeavors of the small. As we fall, the vultures descend down to wrap their talons around the throats of the weak. In the weeks to come, the effects will unravel in front of our eyes. Look into the streets, now paved in a caravan of carcasses who were in search of relief from being paralyzed from starvation. Set down in aggravation, they began to fall. At the vulture's feet, they began to crawl. The vulture's greed is taking its toll, while hatred burns and feeds upon our souls. In the middle of the night, all hope was lost. They swooped down to save their greed. At the cost of our rights, they planted a seed. From the ashes of our bodies that covered the dirt, grew outsourced hope. For nothing did we work for, so no more will we be allowed to be the core of their opportunity. Now, no one is left for these vultures to strike down. Our dead bodies line the ground. Using us as a futile fertilization has left our civilization the forth world.

Corporate Cattle

In the middle of the night, they will rise to power and sit upon the throne. In every passing hour, their every action we condone. The dreadful sight of satisfaction painted on their faces, as we let them feast upon our rights. Elected to destroy the masses, and they have done their best. When anything against humanity is all that passes then we are truly free. We are free to accept what we cannot change. It is a strange thing to think that our shrinking rights were our own fault. We allowed ourselves to follow in the same footsteps that our founding fathers set for us. Though it is seemed as a twisted perception, their misguided conceptions have led us free to be their slaves. As our rights are becoming further concaved, we mindlessly set forth down the same trail. The salt lick lies have contorted to become our truths. We will continue staring at the blank gazes of our kings. We will continue to graze at their feet, stuck at the mutiny of our rights. The force fed ideals have made it impossible for the kings to conceal the fact that we are cattle. We have enthroned them. We have saddled our own backs. The final straw has been thrust into our backs. Justice has been caught without her eyes, as we make our way into the final slaughter.

Take Time To Smell The [Crap]

How many more glasses of piss warm lemonade must we ingest, before we begin to detest the rotted, lemon lies they throw at us? How much more before we realize the world only seems to be peachy, because the rose colored glasses, perched on the bent frames, are rapidly beginning to fade? How long must we sit, with hands tied as they tie the gag around our mouths? How much more time before we are free to speak our minds? How strong is there will to destroy mankind? How many more ice cold pink slips can be served from their silver spoons, from our melting pot? How many more times can we be blamed for their mishaps? How come we all have the time to make them rich, but can never take the time to smell the [roses].

Life only seems peachy, while looking through the fading rose tint now perched on bent frames. The roses are wilting faster than we can absorb the stench of hollow promises.

Soldered

Connected forever to what I have seen

Fused by blood and shortened lies, cast off into the blanket of sea shells. The sweltering emotions, nothing more than dust covered thoughts. Flash flames accosted wills. The thrill of one, outnumbered in detained feelings. The screaming of shredded metal corrupts all that I see. Black and blue, black and red, the painted walls now left for dead. Inside the group, I am now entombed. Inside the land, I am nothing. Led to lead, bleed to nothing more to be bled.

Bound eternally to what they have conceived

Fused by hatred, I am captured by my own. Attack my emotions, blinded by olive colored branches. Colors are bright. Darkness falls, as I have already done. Muzzled noises now brightly shine. Light up the sky that I now detest. Too much vested to ever leave. The screaming metal of the muted defeats have now called my name. Trapped inside my own metal cage, as I drown in dust, water cannot rinse the images from my mind. Help myself with a final bit of what was said.

Never to break away from this that is thought so obscene

Compartmentally Challenged

Inside your minds something went horribly wrong
Empty promises left you empty and you cannot go on
Your words have no meaning they corrupted your brains
Take without asking who cares who it pains
The gray matter is nothing but a vacant shell inside
Searching for truths but all thoughts have died
Your new dark reality has drained your strength
You try to come to grips by any length
Looking for the power that you once cherished
The brain is now numb and all thoughts have perished

Inside your brains you feel something go awry
Regaining your thoughts you can no longer try
With melted brains your words are now mumbled
Over your lies you have already stumbled
Your will to communicate is starting to collapse
Corrosion behind your eyes is drudging up your past
We are forced to agree to the muck and lies
Knowing it is yourselves you now despise
With so many half truths you cannot keep them straight
The time has past for your mind it is too late

Inside your heads you can feel the void
The dark emptiness that has made you annoyed
The retardation of manipulation that you try to display
We are vexed at the mistakes you made that we are forced to pay
The abyss of knowledge has grown too much bear
Stand there without blinking with an obnoxious stare
Falling over backwards as you trip over your concern
Left with nothing inside as your brains start to burn
In all directions you words begin to splatter
Leaving you nothing of your worthless gray matter

A Work in Recess

We are only muddling through another miserable day
Trying to understand just why
Truly it is not for the pay
And another wasted miserable day just went by
They do make it all too easy to immediately up and leave
This shattered system that we let them control
It is for a better life so we are deceived
Just let them stroke your ego as they slowly drain your soul
Funny how they can look at you and grin
They will tell you life is going to change
Patting you on the back as the knife goes in
Seemingly those differences are always out of range

Well another miserable day has now arrived
Again we muddle through another agonizing day of work
New ways to torture your dignity is the best they could contrive
Our patience wearing thin as we are force to watch them smirk
Promises and promises of soon to be reforms
Every bleak morning the self torture we endure
To give in to their specifications we are forced to conform
With every passing moment our spirits begin to break
Working for nothing, the end is for what we hope
This mindless manipulation that I can no longer take
My end is here and I can no longer cope

Economically Sodomized

Now, I probably should hesitate before I ask why you did not lubricate as you found your way inside of the ladies and gentlemen. But as it has been with every administration, we keep the lubrication buried tightly deep inside our own land. Good to know you have our backs, as you stand so far behind. You stab us in the back as you are penetrating our mind. With oil lubrication buried tightly in the ground, you only legislations cause no jobs to be found. Our economy is slipping further out, as your lies slide further in. I mean not to belittle, but you are doing nothing as our jobs begin to whittle down to the slightest thimble of opportunity. So sit upon your throne and judge our actions that you don not condone. As we are all clad in pink slips, out on the street, and no one is left to kiss your feet, remember the ideals that you did believe in. It was in this that our broken backs you did thieve. What you believe to be the just cause, as you pass your outdated laws. The best there is to offer is the marriage of the gays, as a viable blame for the jobs that are slipping out of reach, thrusting away from us, faster than the days. It does seem so odd to deem that this is why we cannot find a job. We broke our backs, so that you can make them tired and sore. How will you get paid when there is no more money for us to pour? Now that you have left this nation completely down sized, who is left for you to…

Sleepless Mourning

I closed my eyes to be awakened, finding my body dieing from the recurring dream. Silently, I sleep. The mistakes have taken their final stake inside my empty heart. The streets are now paved in lies, as my body lies down on the side of the vacant road. The shallow grave of humanity has grown as meaningless as their words. The acidic sky of shame is pouring down on my empty head. The dead thoughts inside can no longer respond. I can do no more than let them drown in their acidic ponds. The strangleholds of their lies have left me too weak to fight back. I open my eyes to return to the sullen dream. I watch as the journey of life has careened out of control. The foul stenches of their lies have wilted my bitter soul. I live in the fear of anticipation of our rights now being set free

The Destitute Streeter

Every night I would watch her walking down the streets. I would admire that sun colored hair, with those auburn streaks. That angel face would light up my dismal nights. She had a smile that was brighter than the stars. Often, I would wonder how far I would go to touch her face. Inside those blue eyes, was the shame she hid inside. Too many days for me to count, I wish I could take that pain away. By the time that night would appear I shut myself off to the world. I locked myself inside my fears. She would drift up and down the same avenues in search of each evening's Mr. Right. With the flower of my heart in full bloom, I could do nothing but wait for another day. Life began to change. No one came for even a moment of her time. I did not realize how full her empty plate had gotten. I could only imagine how rotten she must feel, living with the shame that she found harder to conceal. I wanted nothing more than to know her name, and yet I could never bring myself to ask. I miss seeing that smile that was forgotten, and left in the past. As life took away her clientele, and from one day to the next she could no longer tell. I did nothing to stop her smile from falling. I could see the tears falling from her once bright eyes. So long ago her dignity had been stripped away, and now the economic status was getting worse with every passing day.

Every night I had spent watching those streets for my love, the sun colored haired angel, with those auburn streaks. Now plagued by life, her smile was duller than the view through the morning fog. Bogged down by the self pity, she struggled to keep locked inside. Her eyes glassed over as her patience began to fall. All I wanted was for her to be safe. I wanted to take her off those streets, and learn her name. The way she moved was slowing down and the twinkle in her eyes was completely gone. It was getting much too late for me to save that angel's face. It grew too much of a burden to hide her disgrace. The autumn leaves had started to change, and the failing economy had caused all the jobs to fall. No longer did they have means to look her way. It was obvious to all that her pride had slipped away. I looked out my window and I could no longer see that shining face that had meant so much to me. Her head never again looked up to the sky. I did nothing to get her off those streets. All I needed was some courage for the chance to meet. She no longer could look at my window as she walked by. I was ready and had made up my mind. On a very cold night, I stepped out to find my love. She was walking slowly, with the thoughts of self respect she hoped to regain. I stepped out in front of her to ask her name. In her eyes I could see the pain. I still said nothing.

The final night that I had looked for my love, the once radiant girl now with greasy blond hair and faded streaks. She slowly walked past me sick and tired. I held my breath to rekindle the fire. It was too late, my love was gone. Life got in her way, and I was wrong to think waiting was the right way to act. The simple fact everyone was unemployed gave her boss no choice but to let her go. She faced the ground and made her way to the alley to sit in the dirt. I hurt knowing it was about to end. To the alley, I made my way to save the friend that I had never met. The harder I tried to dismiss it as a lie, the more I could feel it was over. I walked over to find her resting on the ground and the knife still clenched in her hands. Worthless and broken, she felt that she had no other choice to cave. She stabbed her chest, and it was too late for me to save her. I knelt down, holding the knife, kissed her cheek as I said good bye. I missed the opportunity for a proper discourse, abandoned on the streets, the auburn streaks now gone. Her profession was now being outsourced to life. The strife of holding in her shame became too much to bare. The constant agony of despair she let her self go, and I held her until the morning. I was still mourning when she was found. It was to the once bright eyed angel that I was bound. Life killed her but could not take the blame. She killed herself so to free her from the shame.

Run On Emotion

To what extent are we to sit back content with the social deprivation of freedom, while knowing that there is nothing more than starvation and lies in our lives that have become a constant routine to strive for something more substantial than the mediocre existence that has bored us longer than we expected our tattered persistence to allow, while we continue to follow the same lies that our ancestors died trying to protect us from having to neglect our offspring who will have to suffer the same taxing fate which has become too late for us to change, given their constant unwillingness to rearrange the outdated search for empowering their own greed despite our subtle requests to appeal

Work Divided

LOOKING INSIDE OF ME MUCH TO NO AVAIL, I LEFT MY SOUL BEHIND, KNOWING THAT MY LIFE HAS FAILED.

Dark as the shady night allows, my soul slips down into oblivion. Again, I feel the nothing of my life consuming me as I am forced to wake. My life drips down into my slumber's cell as I sluggishly begin to rise. Looking down at my bed, I am unwilling to carry on. It is the daily plight of the soul to drag the heels, kicking and screaming on the way to my demeaning second home. Condone their degrading treatment of everyone, because the voices tell me to. Go inside to set my mind on the daily strife of working. Seeing people has become the first warning sign that life has gone awry. My soul is still set in a coma as I make myself muddle through my day.

I STAND ALONE OUTSIDE MYSELF LOOKING FOR AN ESCAPE. WITH EVERY PASSING DAY, MY HEART SLOWS ITS PACE.

Reminders of failure haunt my every move. Every silent step betrays me. I cannot break free. Regretting the days that I now rue, I smile with a fake laugh. I try to forget my past, but my dead soul has its hands over my eyes. I can't see the future that I have left behind. The dark cloud of life pours its thick cloud over me. I can no longer see why I came here. I detest that I started and I detest that I stayed. It has become harder to see a point to leaving my soul back in that dreary bed. The cold dead feeling of this empty place has me encased inside my own fears. Make my way back home, blocking out their judgmental stares.

CLOSING MY EYES, I TRY TO AWAKE FROM MY DAILY NIGHTMARE. THEIR CONSTANT NAGGING IS STILL RINGING IN MY EARS.

I close my eyes to finally listen to the silence playing in my mind. As the passing time still plagues me and my reality of a mistaken good idea, I rejoin my soul, waking it from it coma. The work day ends sending me to a better place. I rest my head on the pillow that houses my calming thoughts. It takes me far away from the nagging thoughts of my second home. Ripping me the days I now detest, my souls pulls itself back inside of me. My soul is back at home as I close my eyes. The oblivion of night is oblivious to the pain it is set to cause. My jaw drops as I realize that I am once again forced to open my eyes.

ENCASED IN A COFFIN OF CONSTANT REGRET, LIFE HAS LEFT ME TO LOOK AT THE LIFETIME OF NEGLECT.

Well, Lobby for Me

Seems every time we turn around someone is out there with so much to say
We all just sit back as another right is being stripped away
We let the lobbyist lobby day after day
What sounds good for them is what we have to pay

In every passing second, can't help but feel strange
As someone we have never met is telling us to change
And every aspect of our life is starting to rearrange
We just watch as our freedoms get further out of range

More often than not, this is no longer good
You can not do it because they don't think we should
We might be all out of work and a home, if only they could
Tell them to stop, who is to say they would

With every passing second we will shortly not be free
All because they are telling us who we are to be
There is one plaguing question from sea to glistening sea
Why isn't there anyone out there lobbying for me

A Life Vested

I walk the plank and dive into the shark infested waters of life. The chalk outline of my integrity floats past. The water has risen deep. Staring out before I took the leap, I am stuck in the ocean with no relief. I watched my ship set sail. I am waiting for its return. Each in turn, the sharks attack and I fear I am drowning. I cannot wade here any longer. The water has grown to deep and I not strong enough to continue. I have tried for too long to get myself free, but the undertow drags me back under. I am surrounded by water and the bodies of those the sharks had already taken its grasp upon. I am alone. Inside a great amount of water, lie those bodies which have grown too many to count. I am being pulled back under as the waters continue to rise. The shark's fins are coming closer again. I cannot swim away. With every passing day, the water is thicker. It is so much thicker than when I was first forced to walk past the chalk outline of my integrity. Again, I try to swim away. The rising water has me trapped. My ship set sail never to return. I am drowning and the water filled my chest. My life vest was filled with sand. To my debt I shall be forever damned.

Desperation

Again we wake to see the day, mindlessly entering the dismal gray. Burn out as we try to face the unsettling reality that there is no tomorrow, because yesterday has arrived again. Try as we might to derive to a new solution, no longer can we trick our minds to this illusion. Catching ourselves entering another yesterday, for everyday is the same. All of us get paid, to say nothing and just accept the pain. Except, the pain is here again and tomorrow we can all expect the same. Tomorrow will always remain out of range. Everyday is same, this will never change.

The Cabinet Fakers

Lie again my friends as again you let the truth bend with every mixed message that you send. Commence upon the new litigation that the nation does not pay enough in taxation. So, do please spare the aggravation of telling us there is negation to any form of vacation from this way of life. The hardship and strife must be an incredible knife in your side. No easy way to take back those lies, when any form of blame, your cabinet denies. Why change what is already tried and true? Now, my friends, I am at the end. The only helping hands that you lend are the ones that extend to help our jobs descend. Apparently, it is easy to pass judgment on us that the expectation of a decent budget will fix this. But, how quickly you forget that what you said is not quite what you meant. Go ahead, my friends, and pass around the blame in search of any takers. Unless you have forgotten it is you, not us, that are the cabinet fakers.

Betsy's Protection

The broad stripes of protection are shining like stars in the dark blue tint of the night. Despite the neglect of the others whose convictions we fight for, we stand firm in our blood red convictions that all have the right to be free and safe. It is commonplace for us to bring forth the white light. For this is the backdrop of opportunity. Still, they cannot understand, and they still cannot see. It is under Betsy's command, and it is for their protection that we send forth our reflection of what it means to be finally free. So, continuously, we ask that Betsy's blood red convictions and the white light of opportunity stand side by side under the blue of night, and continue to fight for all the stars of the world.

You're Hired

Though I knew that the deficit was on the rise
It still came as such a surprise
To the point, I could not believe my eyes
I thought it was just more printed lies

I rubbed my eyes to change my sight
I just could not believe such a dreadful fright
A note to my boss, I just might
After seeing my job posted, on an auction website.

I called my boss to see if he lied
I could do nothing, I sat there and sighed
My emotions now were taken for a ride
When five foreign countries already applied

A person was hired, who could start today
He'd be there shortly, without delay
Out on the streets, without any pay
Because I lost my job, on that site that I cannot say

Virtually Governed

Robotic leader, void of life. No emotion, no remorse.

Bound by wire, auto responses. Cold and calculated corruption

Automated pain caused our strife.
Preprogrammed notions set off course.

Mass produced circus of circuitry, now set for nuclear eruption

Virtually led into worldwide genocide. No regrets for set decrees

Operating on a system, worldwide scale. Remotely connected by this inner planet virus.

Digtilaly mastered world collaborations, death to all by programmed means

By robotic leaders, programmed off course, massacred system with no one behind us

The grounded wire has been stripped of its rank, the final empty promises never to reboot

Controlling Quality Time In Darkness

I woke up to see the darkness still covering me. It presses the blanket down and holds me to my dreams. With a morning frown plastered on my face, and my body still set for snooze, and inside my mind, I scream as I force myself to rise. Cleaning myself, still willing to sleep, finding it increasingly harder to keep on feet. I start my hell bound chariot and make my way. The sun has yet to rise to begin its day. The stars swoop down holding my will to sleep in place. I look up to see if the sun was ready to offer a morning hello, but it was in vain. The sun is still slouched in slumber as I continue on my way. Sliding into place, I am now home in the ice covered lot. I drop my head as I look to the rust, brown door of my prison home. Clouds pour over the stars. The car is locked, my spirit has not yet risen, and the clouds have fully descended. They have completely entombed my dungeon home. Entering my daily prison, my spirit falls further than the clouds. I walk the shop to stretch my legs, while contemplating the dismal days ahead. Through the glass block windows, the darkness still shines and the sun has still not begun to wake. I begin my day of misery staring at the dismal gray and army green machines. Finally, through the glass blocks, the first groggy beam of light the sun has to offer starts to shine. The smell of my coffee quickly gives way to the stench of burning oil. The pounding metal machines are echoing in my mind. The sun shine is blocked out by the glass blocks. The steam of the burning oil is giving the appearance of the clouds entering my prison. The dark, dank dungeon locks me inside my own mind. The constant clanking metal is making it increasingly harder to think straight. The greasy floor steals my ability to walk. The stagnant stench of oil is becoming more than I can handle, but my day is only half over. I spend my time in quiet isolation. The desolation of a lonely lunch beats the constant beating of the pounding machines. Thirty minutes of daylight and contemplation, before I make my way back inside my prison. Then, it is back to the nagging aggravation of the rest another dismal day. Sliding inside the greasy prison, I spend the passing hours listening to the constant clanking machines. My hands are now cut and bruised and ever so tired. It is moments away from the ending of my daily mental abuse. The pounding seemingly set to cease, as I clean away slivers and grease. The sun is gone, already fast asleep. Night surrounds the subtle sounds of my chariot. Without regret, I no longer forced to listen to the banging metal of my daily prison. Again I drive, blanketed in darkness. Parking on the street, I look to the stars as they mock me with their twinkling lights. I enter my home locking myself inside my mind. I am now set to fall asleep, blanketed by my darkness.

A Gentle Serenity

Bend over backwards, while breaking your back
Beckon you back for another attack
As commoners you came, while they looked for all your cash
Came and went, slipped through the crack
They bent you over backwards, while you were breaking your back
Feel a slight twinge as your wallets attacked
Break your back, feel your cash slip through the crack
Work your life away, and have nothing to show
Watch your life's work slip away
And then it's time to go

Inside An Empty Shell

Listen to the new waves of lies pouring down from an island of corruption. Mountains of mistakes pile higher with each passing lie. In turn, they turn their heads and let us die. We can bleed out oceans for other's creeds, but cannot be set free from ourselves. Put the shell of life to our ears as we listen to lies pouring from their majestic kingdom. The once great pillar of salt has eroded in time. Every mistake we find adds to the blind denial. Again, we have grown too blind to see past the rising tide of greed. Our hands tied together bound in red taped objection to everything but this greed. Allowed to state our objections to everything we have agreed. Listen to the oceans of our tear, stained blood, but never to our own words. The distance between us and their majestic castle is too far to swim. We will drown. Cannot set down the shell, it is all we have left. It is all that remains of what was once great about this land. It is the carcass of truth. It is the skeleton outline of what we once believed. Listen to the lies that lie inside the cadaver of broken promises, while standing on the bones of our principles which have been swept under the rug of trust. Hold the shell to your ears and listen, as we drown in the shallow grave they have dug for us.

Demoted To Perfection

Across the world, the rivers begin to rise. Yet, the world leaders continuously deny responsibilities. As the water grows deeper around their majestic castles, we are left to our devices as we stand at the edge of a new reality, on the ashes of rights. The moats around their castles have grown too deep for us to reach them. On the beach of lies we stand, no longer proud of what we see and are forced to hear. The skeletal outline of our beliefs has grown too frail. The weathered red tape is failing to hold together. The perfect castles they built out of the rising sands of our better days, still look perfect. We are drowning in the lies and mistakes. The oceans of salt, stained blood have grown too thick to swim. We may listen to the shell reminding us how we failed. We have fallen to our knees, staring out into moat of their perfection. The majestic faces can only be seen in the faded reflections. The deeper the oceans begin rise the higher their castles begin to rise. Their kingdoms are perched well above the mountain of their mistakes. Despite our feelings of rejection, the moat they dug between us is proof of their perfection. Time has come to hold our breaths, as we listen to the lies set inside the shell of life. The strife of seeing through the blood of greed kicks us into the moat to feed.

Mistaken Integrity

Mountains of mistakes pile higher across every land, as we drown in the sands of time. We reach out over the cadavers of broken promises but are pulled back under the mountains of mistakes. Without hesitation, the majestic glares down at the sands of our remains. As we have all drowned in the in salt, stained blood, they have nothing left to build on their perched castles. The past shells we listened to have eroded into nothing more than dust. The rug of trust has collapsed under the weight of lies, and has fallen into in the ocean. Emotionlessly, the great reaches out to pull us from the depths of our own inhumanity. However, their efforts are in vain. The moat they have dug for us has swallowed the remains. No more will we swim to the castles. The final drops of our blood and tears have consumed us. We are now the cadavers of broken promises. The world leaders can now look down at the skeletal outlines of their failed beliefs. The mountains of mistakes are now unable to pile up any higher. The denial of our rights has left us to be the carcasses of their truths. As life has passed away, they are left to hold empty shells to their ears. We drowned under the weight of lies and mistakes. The perched castles have begun to fall. Greed has swallowed the world whole. It's too late for an empty integrity

An Avalanche of Suffering

Good times had by all. Watching our lives begin to fall. Despite how many times we call out for help, we are forced to sit on the side of life waiting for the day to come that all their mistakes will be undone. It is becoming way too much to bear, waiting days for someone to care about the pain and tears. The failed life is seen through balling eyes, but never theirs. Slipping through the cracks of life, with our backs against the wall, they have the knife of devastation planted in our sides. We have nothing but their lies to abide to. In time, we will have to do just as they ask and tell us to. Like being encaged in their lies, we are trapped in their new truths. All of what we know is what they tell us to. They respond with nothing but lies and hate for our every word. The most disturbing truth is the knowledge that there is no relief. Mountains of mistakes pile too steep to climb. All the while, they keep trying to slide more into the majestic heap. There is a low light hovering over us inches from our wool covered eyes. Now, our only relief is an avalanche. It is better to be buried alive in the trenches of their mistakes, than it is to live a life suffering from them.

My Slain Sanity

The last breath of my dreams has started giving way to another bitter morning. These are the final calm moments before my daily mourning begins. As it has been for years, I am set to leave my sanctity as I say good bye to my sanity once last time. Each and every day, I wake more reluctantly than I day before. My prior life of happiness has given way. It had fallen under the strain. Reluctantly, I make my way. I try to cleanse away the guilt of having stayed. As I take one last look to my sanity, I can see that it is fast asleep. This time it will remain that way. My daily routine has stripped my pride away. My head drops, as the head of my will to move falls under the guillotine known as work. I pressure myself into believing that waking up was the right decision. It is getting harder these days to trick myself into seeing clearly as the eyes of an insane reality are shattered by the wrecking ball known as work. Through the smirks and judgmental eyes, I now despise what little self respect I have left. It has dwindled down to nothing, eroded under the down pour of lies known as work. Hours pass and the last moments of my daily assassination to my heart have come to pass. I was now set to return to check on my slumbering sanity. I cleanse off the ruse of a life known as work. Then, kneel down and pay my respect to my sanity. In its death, I opened my eyes to see that life is nothing more than work. The harder life becomes, the harder we work to survive.

Holy Cost Paid

The flash of sandy, gray sound lights up an emerald sky.
Sonic heat festering from a devastated ground, in a cloud of fungus, the world dies.
The earth now lined with humanity's remains.
Into the craters of our mistakes, life begins to drain.
Rapidly dropping into the ashes of lives, is the bitter tasting soot of the remnants of lies. A gray matter cloud chokes our will to think, as the devastation of our souls sinks further into an instant oblivion.
Hydrogen oceans blast away our greed, as death greets our souls because we differ in creeds.
A sudden flash of ice covers us in a snow of ash and bones.
There is an instant faith in the hatred that the world now condones.
It has bought us to an instant death.
Without regret, the reaper's grim finger touches the masses.
Everything wilts and burns as the ocean passes. It drowns us in our corruption.
It burns us alive in the worldwide eruptions.
The ravenous fires devour all in its path.
. All beliefs were lost in the aftermath.
Let differing deities be blamed for our mistake.
The earth quakes,
It shatters, and it swallows us whole.
The festering heat devastated our souls.
False beliefs caused all to be lost.
Finally, we have
Paid the holy cost.

Loathe of Bred

Starve and wither, and allow yourselves to die. Encased in your own greed, the world is eating out of your hands. Bread crumb severances for the once revered have become what is left of the neglected masses. Past down homicidal beliefs let us eat the dirt from your shoes, while you suffocate on our ashes. Choke on the death of the wilted lettuce, that you grown just to watch us die. Allow yourselves to drown in the rising yeast of your own guilt. Passing generations die under the forced dieting decrees. We can no longer afford food. You can no longer look to the sky to find the broken talon of the eagle. Its wheat was dropped into the valley of your deceptions. It was buried under the passing generations of short comings. Suffocate on the rotted wheat of your own lies. Choke on your bread crumb greed, as we sever ties with your ancestral strife. Look down form your throne, and watch as the neglected masses, wither and die from loathe of your bred.

Olive Branch

The white flag has been raised, as we fall to our knees. We call out to deaf ears. We surrender to defend our right to live. We already surrendered our right to think. White doves drop from the sky, and grovel in vain. There is no change, piece of mind falls from the broken branches. It crashes to the ground and shatters all hope. The flag pole rusts as you set our flag at half mast. The past repeats as we are again forced to kneel and shatter under the weight of our own mistakes. Without hesitation, we have been left for dead, under the tattered flag of a déjà vu reality. Destiny is destined to repeat, as the rotting branches further decays. The days are the same and our white flag has only been seen by the blind eyes of our own injustices.

Beheaded

How quickly you were able to push for a change. You lounged around complaining about your rights being taken. While they had the eyes of Justice already gouged, you never once thought about the freedoms you have taken for granted. All of your rants have fallen on deaf ears. Not once did you realize that you caused your own despairs. As you sat upon your polyester thrones, the soapbox couches nestled warmly in your homes. You claimed we were no better off than any foreign land. You sat locked in silence, screaming under a new tyrant's command. You were as quick to judge as you were to complain about another privilege of yours that was now being slain. It was easy to lead you to believe that we had fallen under tyranny. At the same time, you had forgotten an apparent irony. I tried my best to audibly state every word you said. Despite your opinions I still kept my head.

IV

A Voided Personality

Calm the Storm

Winds rip through, like the breath of a dragon on a cold winter night. Burning for hours and a week. I'm weak for now, as the rains pour like a steady stream horizontal with the sky. Brutal floods, the flowers wither and then die. Like a waterfall eroding the mountainside, winds force the rain aside. A woman walks slowly, staggering through the night tempest, worse she claims to have seen. Cold, blistering fingers, sheets of ice, glass blankets on the streets. River up ten feet or more, raging seas, attack, then soar. Daylight stolen by thick clouds inches from the ground, shadows and darkness disguise the town. People dash from car to house, soaked, bruised, battered, and abused. Thunder and lightning, hail and danger, who will come to end this menacing stranger. We were never warned this blow would attack. Now who will come to get it off our backs? Who will come to calm the storm??

Bitterness bites your purple hands of pain, leaving you out in the rain and snow. You are old enough to know it was cold. Layers of ice covers the grass, as piercing winds rip through your body like cries of the children thrown from their homes in a downpour. Rains cover your vision and your dreams. The vicious cold air attacks you from all sides. Your nose beat red, as are your eyes. Clouds hovering over the ground block the sun, which has vacated the earth for the winter. Hail bounces off of you as you stand in seclusion, alone with your confusion. This is a never ending blow, or least the final one. You were never warned about it. Now who will come to calm the storm??

The Sweating Coffin

I feel as if I am carrying an added weight inside me. What is this feeling deep inside me, which is weighing me down? It feels cold and empty. I can't break this agonizing feeling deep inside my chest. I feel myself moving fast. I feel colder as I go. I do not know where I am headed. Outside, my existence feels as cold and empty, as the added weight inside me grows heavier. My new place of rest seems so final. Great pain and sadness fills this room. I do not understand this feeling. Suddenly, I taste salt water from a warm touch. It's gone, the room now feels empty as the added weight inside grows. Again, I feel myself moving. The walls are closing in around me, I feel as if I am dropping. I am so scared and alone. It's dark. It's Peaceful.

Mental Lock Down

Time has come and gone. It has left me standing alone. I have chained myself to fear, I cannot brake free. I am trapped inside my mind, as I am passed by an eternity of lies. Every excuse I can make, I cannot escape the self abuse I make myself feel. It is unreal to think of better days, I am alone inside of myself. Life cannot set me free. The dismal reality behind my eyes chains me to the pain I caused the world. I close myself off, so that I may offer an escape to everyone else. Placing my mind on a shelf, I close my eyes. No more can I go on knowing my mind is locked away, waiting for the sun to shine a light on where I need to be. I cannot see a better day. With no relief, I lock myself away. The key has been lost forever and at any cost I will forever turn away. I never care to find the key to my mind. I am safer knowing that my mind is tightly locked away. Everyone is safe in the comfort of me being locked away. The dismal days I have set myself in, will be my life. Their lives will never change. The pain I caused will never again be seen. I locked my mind away to free you from the strange dream of my dark reality. No more can I offer refuge, so no more will I refuse you the right to be free from my mind. In time, I hope the world will see my life is better locked inside. No more may I exchange my emotions with an unseen reality. The world is now free, and I have the gate of my mind tightly closed. It is for the world, that this is the path I chose. For eternity, I will remain, locked down, deep inside of me.

The Miracle of the Vampire's Curse

Through the night, I see a frown
A nightmare of a killing clown
I see blood stain on the floor
The life of evil is full of gore

Hear the music of my past
Broken limbs trapped in a cast
Walls with open skulls
Death and Danger in our falls

Feel the heat of the Vampire's bite
Now it's over no chance to fight
Shadows of demons upon my bed
Visions of Hell all through my head

Pain and suffering corrupt my dreams
Strangle hold stifle my screams
Tears come out as you are forced to cry
No chance to live or even try

Two holes upon or within the neck
All your life is such a wreck
The Vampire's curse is upon your heart
Your life has been torn apart

Your only chance is to pray
You hear voices but don't know what they say
It's your only chance to be saved
It's too late the way has been paved

Poetic Pain

Every night, I fight the demons that are in my sight, trying to do what is right, but my mind is demented, tired, and tormented. Heaven is my incentive to rid my mind of the inventive pain I have made. In the night, as I lay my head upon the pillow, weeping like the tree outside my window, hoping that life does not get the best of me. I know it, for I am ill. I popped another pill, but I am alive still. My breath begins to sting, as I inhale someone else's dream. I cannot help but to scream. My mind is plagued with fear, corruption, and mental tears. I need another laced drink, to help me think. Outside my room, all is normal, but I can't cope.

The Screaming Earth

I am the earth, and I am sore
I am a shattered dream, like a window

I am total obliteration, I am war
I am a scream, muffled though

My screams are muffled, by piercing cries
I try to help, but I am impotent

Death has struck here, my body lies
I am the earth, I am omniscient

I was once powerful, I was the earth
I was once beautiful, but that was at birth

Humans are bugs to me
They have amputated my last limbs

I let the bugs live, and they stay alive
I am glad I did, because now they have died

repressed seclusion

Send me far away and leave me to find joy inside my mind. Lock me up so tightly that my end I might find. Drop me down a well far enough to perceive that that my thoughts were not really mine to believe. Quiet my words that I may hear the voices of what has disturbed me for too long. Force me aside such that I have the time to look inside all that I have wronged. Cage me inside the pain I caused so many. Darken my heart's eyes so it sees no more of any. Board me inside the crate of self created misery. Shut me out from the world and let me dwell in self loathing and self served pity. Cover me in dirt so I may suffocate in my perception's tomb. Lower me into limbo and trap me in a perceived reality of gloom. Chain me to my mind in an effort to suppress delusions. Free me from my mind's life such that I may separate from its repressed seclusions.

Drain Pipe Dreams

You are slipping down the pipe, further into the abyss.
Your thoughts drown, as your empathy is set to cast off, and apathy rides the wake back in.
As your mind becomes flooded with despair, you fish for less painful memories;
All of which have been lost at sea.
The agony is pouring over your happier days.
The cloud of shame has set in.
Again, you feel nothing, as your dignity is washed away by the pain you caused yourself
searching in vain for nothing more than more questions.
Sit there alone, as all hope is now watered down into another drain pipe dream.
The quick fix was only plum to the septic thoughts of your cynical mind.
The valve of your procrastination has been opened and there is no shut off in sight.
You now dwell, drowning in the abyss of your own misery, under the sands of time,
And wait for the tide to roll back a better control to your distorted reality.

The Summer Sunned

The flowers of lies are now in full bloom. The warm air of disillusion has blown down forever left to loom. Scorching thoughts of what is real has slowly burned away. The metal frame of reality has melted another day. Live in the illusion of what I see and the hidden voice that I believe. Again, I am tricked by what has shined. Again, I see the fire of the mind's lies that burns brighter than the sun. Summer is an illusion. It is easily confused with reality. My true reality still rests in hibernation. It is set in slumber from the lullaby of the voices within. The mind's lies are hotter than I thought. My boiling blood has destroyed my will to breathe. I block out the summer sun to seize the day, but cease to move. The sweltering summer has taken its final leap from its hibernation. My will burns in a constant coma. I now realize that damned to be alone with the voices.

Sad Death

My heart is pained, by the lack of love
The burning earth, that flaming dove

All this madness may be deemed as crass
But it's not a trend, it just won't pass

Pain and suffering is more than a scare
Stronger killing weaker, it's just not fair

So much injustice has been a plague
I am so indignant to this violent rage

Never ending, without any trust
The earth is condemned to corruption and rust

We are all just wasting time
Looking for answers we know we won't find

Felt for you, now I have died
Wept for you, too many tears for you I've cried

If I remained alive, maybe I could have helped
I know the pain; it's something that I have felt

Living in this life, alone without friends
We're living a cycle that never ends

Entrapped

Tightly locked inside myself, I cannot break free. Repetition entombs me inside myself. The vicious cycle of life has chained me inside my own mind. No longer will I search for freedom that I will never find. Withdrawn from the world forced away by my constant mistakes, I must distance myself. Yet I find no escape from the self torture. It is a well deserved fit for the lives that I have taken down and devastated. I have given myself no other choice but to lock myself away inside numbered days. Again, the soft smiles of emptiness are smiling at me. Each smile knows of the grave that I have dug for myself. I possess the sheltered mind tightly locked inside the grave, which is growing by the day. Freedom is lost, now that I am shackled to my mistakes. The key of life has been buried far away. Give in to the repetition there is no change in sight. There is no change. Live out my mistakes and repeat. Give in to the defeat. I am chained to mindless repetition. Live inside my own mind. I am entrapped by lies and deceit. Entrap myself. For no more, will I be free for their happiness. I set my mind free. It is the only way that they can see that happiness is not real. No longer can I deal with the mistakes. I can feel my mistakes taking over my mind. I believe in the lies. I despise myself for being and being who I have become. Life is nothing more than my grave. To lies, I will remain enslaved.

A Second of Time

How quickly it all changes, the strange rearranges
It becomes a distorted reality contorts to pointless efforts.
How rapidly life can turn to pointless efforts.
It conforms to the brutal perception
That the empty reality is becoming our conception
The emptiness never fades, it just jades our existence
Nothing
Of
Our
Life
Remains
All in
A Second of Time

Stagnated To Dementia

The stagnant stench of disillusions devours my sanity. The reality of lies has again forced a bitter hand. I can no longer command my mind not to despise myself for becoming who I am. Again, I am tricked into believing that which I digest is actually the truth. I detest conceding to the lies. I detest knowing that I have been allowing them to alter my perceptions, and watch as again my reality dies. The heart of truth has begun to fail. I lie there mindlessly and do nothing as my clear thoughts are impaled. My sanity slips as it rips itself open, trying to bleed out the lies. The mind goes limp, no longer strong enough to hold on. Rational thoughts are now long gone. Their misleading intentions have spent too much time feasting on my better judgment and clarity. The strangle hold of apathy is choking my mind. I can no longer follow the path of pain that their lies have caused. No one cares how hollow my life is. I am now caused to be locked tightly inside the confines of my mind. The rage has left me with paralyzed eyes. I am now blind to truth and actuality. My reality despises me for believing their misleading notions. It hates me for becoming who I have become. Oceans of lies pour over my mind, suffocating the truth that hides inside my mind.

Brain-Be-Gone

Why have a mind of doubt
What is it all about
What have I done wrong
Why can't my Brain-Be-Gone

Why have a mind of strain
What causes all this pain
What is the reason I can't go on
Why can't my Brain-Be-Gone

Why have a mind of stress
What causes all this mess
What is the reason I can't get along
Why can't my Brain-Be-Gone

Why have a mind of hate
What is the cause of this state
What have I done wrong
Why can't my Brain-Be-Gone

Why have a mind of confusion
What is the cause of this resolution
What is the reason I can't go on
Why can't my Brain-Be-Gone

Why have a mind of despair
What is the cause of my lack of care
What is the reason I can't get along
Why can't my Brain-Be-Gone

Caustic

God please take my hand and get me far away. I just can't take the pain today, the caustic cancer that plagues my brain. Their constant contradictions, their lies I cannot control. There are violent repetitions that are dividing inside my brain. Follow the drastic dropping of reality, the desecrations, of my perceptions. My mind can no longer cope with their deceptions. Dark dank cell, blacken with each passing of the cold days. Continuously, they keep taking me down, pretending to care that I despise myself. The cautious care they take in good measure to inquire about my caustic mind.

The Lobotomy of Morbid Pain

Again I find psychosis setting in,
I grab the knife, and it is time to begin
Mental mutilation, the defecation of a mind
I want to stab you in the heart, while I am ripping out your spine
Shooting you in the throat won't cure my pains
I want to bash in your head and devour your remains.

Dementia is choking on my mind
Feasting on your inside with so much more to find
For your flesh is my insatiable need
I will cut and slice just to watch you bleed
Cut off your head to see what's inside
Shave off your skin and then let you die.

I had found so much beauty with so much hate.
The doctors came to desecrate
They knocked me out with a potent pill
I am chained to a bed, I am feeling ill
I am not to sure just what they have done
Now I am just sitting in a chair and feeling numb

The Schizophrenic Realization

The surreal thoughts of insanity are setting in. My mends but then bends to every voice I hear. My perceptions are altered and I cannot hold reins on my conception that every choice I made may have been in inventive illusion. I am becoming increasingly paranoid and disillusioned. I can see clearly that world hates me, and my corrupted imagination is nothing more than a fascination with the negation of lies that the voices tell me to feel. As I reveal my deceptions, there is a connection to the voices I can no longer conceal. I can see clearly more and more as my visions begin to blur. To each mistaken thought that my mind conjures, I find myself starting to concur. The fear is setting in again that my tired mind cannot be spared. Darkening of the days as the pain mounts inside my brain, and no more hope I can regain. To the voices I did surrender, for I can longer wish to suffer. To them I give in. I can't take the pain, I give.

The Numbing

Masterfully, I can feel my mind slip away. I can no longer determine night from day. I listen to the voices destroying my every thought. Silently I am sitting, staring off, waiting for the emotions to fade as my mind had years before

Oh feel nothing, and be set free. Dark and cold as the summer sets in ice
I am stuck with my own devices

The numbing of emotions as my mind slides down into an obvious oblivion

Hell Inside Me

Dark clouds had begun to pour in, like a steady waterfall hovering over the ground. Like those clouds, the temperature began to fall. The entire earth slowly froze over and all of life ceased in just a second of time. I watched, frozen in time as life died. I could do nothing but watch. My first thoughts were of reasons of why I was being spared. Then, like a recurring nightmare, I begin to see more clearly. All of life, faded away. I was stuck alone watching as everything I have grown to know froze in time. Darkness surrounded me and I was left with nothing more than memories of the better times of my life. Each began to drift away never to be seen again. I fell in to a deep sleep, hoping that when I wake, it would all be over. However, as I woke up, cold and alone, I could see that life was unchanged. It was still froze in ice. It was still as bleak and as dismal as I left it.

I tried to move, but my arms and legs were frozen. I tried to hold my breath, but something kept drawing in air. No chance I could die and all the memories of good times had walked away. Painful memories kept replaying inside my mind. I was not being blessed and saved. I could see this even more clearly now. I was being cursed for the shame and pain I brought forth to this life. I was being punished for all the lies I spread like the wild fire that I began to pray for. I tried swallowing the desolation and despair, but instead I choked on the happiness I once felt; the happiness of knowing that my lies ruined all of life. Desperation trotted off in to the sunset. I was free to feel the numbness begin to set. I could do nothing. I stared off into the abyss that was once life and civilization. My eyes burned at the images of the hate and shallow truths I brought forth to this life.

Trapped, I walked in circles in side my mind. My legs could not keep up with me. I was running to a better life. My legs set in ice, they were unable to cope and I felt them die. My body fell over, and I looked up to the dark clouds. I wanted to find light, but there was nothing but the dark clouds. My heart steadily began to race. My mind traveled in hundred directions, as my heart pounded faster and faster inside my chest. The life that I grew increasingly to detest has now become too much of a burden. I began to panic. The clouds began to disappear. Temperatures began to rise. The ice began to melt. Life had started to come back, as I felt my life slowly begin to drift.

I closed my eyes just as the last bit of life was reborn. It was now shroud in the brightest of lights. I could see the smiles and hear the laughter. Legless, I laid on the ground staring into the light. I tried to move, but fell over and looked down into the deepness of my abyss. I could see how cold, dark, and empty it was. I knew it was a matter of time. I closed my eyes, and made one feeble attempt to get up and start anew. As expected, I never did get on my feet. I simply fell over, and listened to the laughter as my body dropped in to the deepest well. After I had landed, the darkness consumed me. I looked up to the light, but suddenly I was blinded by the dirt being poured over me. Life dropped me down into the abyss, laughed at my screams, and buried in dirt at the bottom of the well. Suddenly, memories of the haunted life I lead destroyed anything left that was good. Soon after this, I felt hot. I felt hotter. I realized I had never felt such pain. I opened eyes and found myself perched on pile of muddy rocks. There was nothing here, but rocks and burned bodies. Flashes of flames poured from a red river. I begged for death, but felt my heart getting stronger. As the strength of my heart grew, so did my will to die. For the rest of eternity, I remained. Begging for death, but lived on forever.

The Invisible Companionship

She stood by me when I was afraid. She consulted my assaulting mind. She placed her hand upon my heart, and whimpered an outrageous ballad from an old book. She told me what was I was to do, to be truly free. I forgot what it was I was to do. Who is she? Is she friend or foe? Is she just an imposter my mind created to reveal my inner thoughts? Help! I cry for help. What is it I must do? Now, I know. So I did what it was I was to do. Though, it has not happened quite yet. It is confusing in a way that is awkward and baffling. How is it we are free in our minds, our souls, and even in ourselves? She is back now, and I am gone. I am at the place I was once before. So many times, I was never helpful.

Cold Aftergloom

Thoughts keep you entombed in the desolation of the cold afternoon. Set in the ice of isolation. You peer to the pier of anticipation, hoping to drown your new day of despair. Look out into the ocean, set to cast off the feelings that your emotions left behind. You cannot quite cope with your heart's deceptions being frozen in time by the frosty air of reality. The chilling realization sets in that your emptiness is setting in, like icicles forming in your mind. The bitter cold bite of the midday digests your will to move. Watch as your last love of life is stolen by a breeze. It has left you nothing left to prove, so you fall upon your knees. You quietly contemplate the meaning of your strife, as the sun gives way to the mist of uncertainty, which has become your nights. Rest your head on your tear soaked pillow, as another desecrated day, which like your life, has begun to decay. The mist of uncertainty chokes your unheard sighs, while you rest you head on a salt stained rock, and fall asleep cursing the merciless skies.

The Evening Mist

You try to sleep off the thoughts of a better time, try to cast them far aside. The mist of uncertainty befriends you, now the only thing at your side. The haunting past of better days are condensing in the stream. As the evening skies begin to darken, you slip into hibernation, unable to dream and the will to carry on slowly begins to wean. You can feel the shadows of the sullen sky, while the nights of missed opportunities still won't let you die. While tiny thinning beads of rain are thrust in, you try to drown out the pain. You know under another sullen sky, you will find the desolation of the sunrise, but your body still won't die. The stars begin to scatter each in their own direction, mimicking your life's ambition, suffering such dissections. Like the stars, your dreams are blocked out by the evening fog. Sit in ice cold isolation, as the light of the moon and the desolate sun go their separate ways.

Desolate Sunrise

The pier of emotion was shorter than you anticipated, as you walked your thoughts to dissipate into the unknown. On the edge of the horizon, you sit down to greet the new day, waiting for the night to fade. You are waiting for the new day to swallow you, as your life already had. You look up to the pathetic sun, which is looking a bit more sad. Stare up to the last of the stars. They are as far away as your dreams. Watch the waves carry your ambitions by. As the suns yellowing reflections, is reflecting the sullen sky. The warmth of the suns rays heats up the memories of better days that are now long gone. Just sit in isolation wondering where you went wrong. Like your life, the sun is beating down on you, leaving your dignity to drift out into the sea. Your integrity slowly begins to drown, as the sun's apathy, boldly knocks you down. Whirlpools of emotions are now distorted from the sun's reflections. As you sit and wait for your life to stop spinning out of control. Just stay there wading as the new day steals the final piece of your soul. You swim back to salt stained rock, the tear soaked pillow that you slept on the nights before. As another mourning passes and still no relief to improve cold afternoon, better take your final breath

Hollow Be My Shame

I sit alone in the stagnant stench of disillusions. The sweltering darkness is heating up the pain I cause. It is growing increasingly hard to face the fact that I caused so much emptiness to so many people. Yesterday's shattered dreams are leaving shards of painful glass memories and destroying them inside my mind. I can feel every broken thought slicing away my happiness. The realization of the pain I cause is repeatedly punching my mind's eye. As I slowly begin to drift into the altered perceptions. What I perceive is nothing more the world's walls closing in on me. I can feel it crushing my spirit. I am consumed and devoured by the insatiable appetite of my own mistakes.

I realize that my mistakes are destroying the loves of everyone I know. It is my self hatred, caused by my short comings, that the world will never understand just how tightly the strangle hold of despair has gripped a hold of me. It is pinning me down, down into the darkness. I can no longer see clearly enough to escape the living hell I have caused this world. The cold, callous way I have treated everyone is biting back on my soul. It is beating me down further and faster everyday. There are no good thoughts left to hold on to. I have forced my hands to go limp as my mind had so many years ago.

The mind I created has nothing left to offer. It has melted away from years of knowing the mental anguish I cause the world. I regret knowing the anguish. I regret understanding it. It was easier to cope when I was blind to reality. The dark pain I caused to everyone is kicking me around. I am weak, I grasping for my final breaths, but they are as elusive as my will to live. I struggle to come to grips with my past mistakes, but slide down too far into the night that I cannot wake to envision a better life.

Finally, I realize that my shame has grown too much. No one is safe as long as I have the power to destroy them. My mistakes have ruined the lives of everyone close to me. It is crushing me down as my eyes twitch from the nerves of knowing what a monster I have truly become. There is no escaping the lies. There is no escaping the pain. I have devastated the entire world with my thoughts and actions. There is nothing left inside me. I ripped a void as I wake every morning to regret my mistakes. I wake in mourning because I have awoken.

Cement Shoes

I feel like I am falling.

Flashes of my life, visions zooming past my eyes
Through past memories.

They are from beyond my reality.

I can see my pain and struggles.
I see glimpses of the elusive triumphs.

Down I go into oblivion
Down I go into a new existence
Down I go into nothing

The only memory I have left is the one
that brought me
Down here.

It is empty at the bottom
But no more than at the top

My life was a cloud.
It dissipated
It rained out my hates and my fears.

Finally, I am
Happily
At
Peace.

Riverdead

In the distance, I saw my dreams. They set sail and left me weak. I watch them on the horizon as I sink down into the abyss. I begin to drown in a river of lethargy. I feel content in the empty feeling of nothing. My mind twists as I struggle to get free. I slide into the oblivion of the deep sea. I allow myself to relax enough to accept the fact no future is seen and my past was a distant memory. A limbo of lies is surrounding me, entombing in the vacant sea. I am weak. I am engulfed in an overwhelming amount of apathy. I am alone inside the waterfall of my mind. Memories of better days are slipping through the quicksand of time. I dove into the emotionless ocean of despair, submerging myself in hopes to be free. I am alive, but my soul is dead. The listless sea has taken me deep. I am at the bottom, sitting and chained to my mind. In pain, but the leaches are feasting on my will. The ship of my integrity and dignity has set sail. I failed to prevent it from being filled with the water of my nightly tears. I sat there at the bottom of the sea. I am alone, but it was my choice to set my ambitions free. I freed myself in time to see my dreams drown and my emerging apathy dry out my shelled life.

Limbo

Life and death, I am stuck between my dreams. Again, I find that I cannot face the days and nights, any more than I can face the screams. Silent voices stuck in my head. I dread the thought that I am set to remain in the cesspool of reality. It drains my will to move, to be stuck in this groove. A broken record of self hatred and broken dreams replays inside my mind. I find that I cannot live, and I cannot die. I try to move, but life has trapped inside this little shell. I fell for the lie that there was more. The horrible feeling of being trapped has left me listening to the voices telling me stay, pushing me away. I cannot break free. I see my past and the future looks the same. Trying in vain to see a better way, my veins fill with regret. I met my end, but I began again.

Life and death, I am stuck between my dreams. The screams are louder, as my judgment clouds. Violent thoughts, of self preservation, I do not deserve to live. I give up my end to send a warning. The mourning I feel will pass. It will begin again. I look to my future, but it looks as if my past is still there. The ill feeling of what I revered has set me entombed inside of my life. I look for a better way, but night and day is still the same. I wake to my dreams flashing before my eyes. I lie down at night and fight the repetition, but life gets in the way. I stand tall, to fall from being knocked back down. As life frowns in my direction, I can see today is yesterday's mirrored reflection

Life and death, I am stuck between my dreams. Choking on the deafening screams has left me breathless. This senseless void inside my mind makes me wonder if I can find peace. At least, I know that the mistakes, that I have made, have placed me in a life that will eventually set me free. If only I can open my eyes before my body dies. Inside my regrets, I silenced the voices that trapped me. All I can see is the emptiness of being stuck between my future and my past. At last, I realize that I am in limbo. I can choose between winning and loosing my mind. In this repetition, I will find peace.

Life and death, I am stuck between my dreams. Silent voices stuck in my head have left me to dread falling asleep. I keep locked inside my mind trying to find my way out. Every night and day may look the same, but my veins pour a will to live. I will not give in to the limbo life, that my mind has trapped me in. Despite my years of self caused sorrow. I can stand here and see tomorrow. Yesterday has lied down in the past. At last, my repetitions are starting to subside.

Life and death, I am free to dream. My screams have blocked out the voices inside my head. I no longer dread living. Life is more forgiving since I closed my mind, and listened to the glistening thoughts of a warm freedom. I planted my mind firmly far away from the days that locked me to myself. Upon a shelf inside my mind, ends the dream of life and death.

Full From the Moon

During the day, I am just a normal man
Avoiding my thoughts with whatever I can
Hoping the night will never get to disperse
Ever so hungry, but I must fight my curse

While during the day, I can just stare at the sun
Contemplating all the harm that I've ever done
In the evening, I become a deadly beast
On anything in my path, I'm forced to feast

I curse the sun, as it begins to descend
Knowing that the moon will come and bring their end
Night comes, devouring what's left of the day
I can feel my heart as it starts to decay

As night starts to fall, hatred fills my cold veins
With nothing human left, my soul slowly drains
I look to the sky, so that I can curse the night
Knowing that I am now a dreadful sight

Devastation and death are now forced to loom
I'm a murderous beast altered by the moon
With no concerns to others or the aftermath
I violently consume all in my path

Catering to my appetite's last command
Following its course and every demand
I have no concern, when is the start of dawn
Again, I feast until all is dead and gone

The moon falls without any form of warning
I fall to my knees, cursing the new morning
My body collapses into the stained mud
Tired and sore, I am left covered in blood

I'm wishing for the death of my appetite
I have no more will to survive, I can't fight
Looked to the wretched sun, that I now detest
I took this silver bullet, to my own chest

The Silenced Shadow

Slipping in silence, your shadow makes its way. It sets out searching for a better way, but something slows its stride. As it cried out for help, every word it calls out falls on deaf ears. As usual, your fears have left you to sleep through the struggle of your shadow's constant plight. As you slept, it sets its sights on a more promising simplicity. Its life just seemed harsher with the passing of the days. In searching for a better place, it stops in the vicinity of death's door. Somehow, it still refuses to enter. It never ceased to see a need to survive. Still alive, you sleep as your shadow slithers past the deception that passes in front of its eyes. With every street it passes, your shadow realizes so much time has been spent concentrating on defeats. So much time had been invested detesting the negative effects of life. It neglected to search for a better way. Momentarily, it suffocates on ashes of its own insecurities. Curiosity about a better way leads your shadow to another place. Disgraced by its own mistakes, it hesitates to continue. Silently, it stops and stares up to the sky. The shadow can no longer stalk the cause of its strife. One last time, the defeated shadow rifles through the last of your dismal thoughts about your life. As the sun slows its slumber, your shadow's silhouette has yet to come to grips with its demise. You wake up just long enough to see the last glimpse of your life pass in front of your eyes.

Down

An inept ability to see the least bit of clarity inside my distorted reality has become my days. From the lack of better ways, I have grown quite fond of the way my perception fades with every passing week. Though it does seem bleak and dismal, the weak voices are becoming a surreal serenity for me. The choices that I have made had led to my own demise, but it was not my fault. There is an assault on my mind, by the seemingly weak voices that apparently only I can hear. They have become more boisterous than they were years ago. My constant fears of confusion about what is real have taken its final toll. I listened to the passing madness trapped inside my frail mind. I find comfort in lacking memories of my past. I stagger blindly through haze of my dismal reality. Life has seen its darker days, as have I. The voices are calling louder. The amount of clouds has grown taking hold of my soul. My downtrodden eyes have fallen to the ground, they no longer care to look up to the misleading sky. I am trapped. Lately, the choices I have made have been dictated by voices screaming in my brain. I cannot find the meaning in the insane life I lead anymore. I need nothing more than to be set free. I have punctured my ears, but still hear the muffled screams. I pried out my eyes, but my vision is still filled with life's distorted reality. It seems that I will be forever confined to my inept ability to see the least bit of clarity inside my distorted reality.

Therapy Addiction

Confined tightly to my addictions, I can take solace in the diction. I thrust my words like a knife slicing away my mind. Battling the emptiness, I fill the pages with the scripted messages that heal my spine. The book of my life binds me to my mind. I am the subject that covers my soul and softens the words of my hard, covered life. With my table full of my mind's corrections, I can seed the contents of my pages have been filled with lies. My broken spine has sentenced me to this darkened chapter of my life. My medication is nothing more than failed diction, and a deletion of my objections to the strife that I have caused others as well as myself. Through the words, I can read between the lines. I find that I was the true curser of my own mind. Again I find that, written in the sands of time, I have prescribed the cure for my own mind. With the contents set on the table of my life, the blank pages and the pen that I have often used as the knife to cure my mind, I am set to take care of me in this time of quiet reflection. My words have become the best cure, my addiction's therapy.

Forced Levels of Offensive Devastation

Suffering from the sounds of thunder, ringing in the chaos of my distorted mind, I cannot find
peace. Flashes of lightning zip past, lighting up my confusion and emptiness. They are no longer
buried inside the back of my consciousness. I am no longer conscious as I
am drowning inside, as the water rises above my head. Pouring down of emotions,
I am pulled under the undertow of despair. Flash flooding desperation, the
nations are cover with liquid death. Without regrets, life is swept under an
under tow of mass destruction. The rising water pulls life further under,
drowning out any thought constructions. Crashing lightning sparks the
ground, flashing of fire's devastation. Surrounded in a swamp of our
regrets, torrential torment rinses our tears away, inside another
week of rain. Life's last breath begins to drizzle out.
Rushing water drowning out in mass devastation,
cast inside our sudden starvation to survive.
Submerging wills fall under, as the
corrosion of life begins to over flow.
We have been forced
inside a net of moral
erosion, we will
drown
in
the
depths
of
our
own
mistakes

The End of Writer's Block

The dust covered pen has been left for dead. It has been untouched and undisturbed right where it had been set so long ago. It faces the now yellowing pages with a single drop of ink. This is not the beginning of a thought, but the end of the ability to think. It is the single, last reminder that no more thoughts can be seen. Walk past the body of your cold, dead pen set on top of the yellowing pages. Remind yourself of your failure. No more words, they have withered down into nothing more than a recurring nightmare. Let it plague your now emptied mind. The ink slowly bleeds out on to the now yellowing pages. The stains of your failure soak through the emptiness. It reveals itself for the world to see. Now, the point of the pen can only point out how stained and tarnished your abilities have become. The tarnished pages are an expression of your life's short comings and nothing more. The pen's thick dark blood perfectly reflects how dark and unclear your thoughts have become. The dust thickens in the ink as another dream is left for dead on the side of the road of your consciousness. Set your head down, and rest as the cold dead pen had done years before. Allow yourself to be free from the mental grip of the stained, yellowing pages. Come to grips with another failed dream. Scream quietly and die, like the unused pen. Be consumed by your failure, and then rest your mind one last time. Slip away and rest from the dream. When your thoughts no longer bleed out of the dieing pen, then the time has come to give. The time has come to become the cold, dead pen.

V

Leave the opinions to the *Prose*

Handshakes

There comes a time in a person's life that their eyes open. They begin to see the world as it truly is. For many, it is already too late to change. The perception that life eventually gets better is always easier to stomach than the reality. Regardless of age, race, or any other man made classification, the true reality is that life sucks. Some argue immigration reform is the answer. However, it is not. As we pump an increasing number of American jobs into foreign markets, an increasing number of foreign people pump into America. Apparently, jobs are not the only problem. It is probably more prudent to look at the world instead of just domestic mishaps. The true problem facing the entire planet is greed. The majority of people can no longer afford to get to the job they are now set to loose.

Globally, political masterminds and CEOs have worked hand in hand building an economical surplus for themselves. They have seen to it that when forced to reduce their own staff, they will still live like kings. Corporations are doing an excellent job of shutting down every small business they can. Meanwhile, governmental officials are leading the way to worldwide bankruptcy. Middle America, as well as middle anywhere, has eroded down to near extinction. Perhaps, social classes had gotten out of hand. Rather than have three independent economical structures, middle class was broken down to an additional three classes. It must have been quite confusing distinguishing between so many tiers. In order to minimize the confusion, corporations and world leaders, all over the planet, realized they needed to eliminate the tricky part. Sadly, the level that has the most headaches for them has now become the center of attention for the rest of us. By taking middle class out of their vocabulary, they realized there was no longer any confusion.

However, they could never possibly foresee an uprising in poverty, homelessness, or crime. Their researchers have made wonderful achievements in doing nothing in foreshadowing the effects of global depression. It is not their fault. Never, in the history of their lives, has there been a depression of such a magnitude. Sure, every country hits a pitfall. Never has the pitfall hit everyone at once. Thankfully, future world leaders and any corporations will have a basis to do research on. On the other hand, as we all starve to death inside our cardboard homes, they will no longer have anyone to research. Then again, when the world is unemployed, no one is going to being making cardboard anymore.

As the two brain trusts are shaking hands, our hands are too tired to shake. Well, except unless one can suffer delirium tremors from food withdrawal. Perhaps, time has come for them to shake our hands, apologize for protecting us, and begin to look at where to draw the line between greed and common sense. We can shake their hand, accept their apologies, and rebuild our futures. The economic problems are no longer national problems. They are global problems. As such, they should be treated globally, and not nationally. If the world leaders and big businesses would stop helping each other and begin helping us, the world would become more prosperous. More efforts to help each other would in turn help themselves. By placing focus on building each other's economy, instead their own, all nations will become wealthier. By shaking hands with enemy countries, wars can cease and we can be wealthy, both monetarily and mentally.

Fed And Fed Up

Life never seems to amaze me. It is a constant merry-go-round that has gradually spun out of control. As I look at my own life, I am shocked at how it mirrors life in general. It started out great, and somewhere it fell apart. It is funny how those infamous, mystical powers that be can calmly kick you in the metaphoric scrotum while you sleep. Silently, I go about my day. Behind, the scenes karma is doing what it does best, stabbing me in the back. This is the bad kind of karma. You know the type. More than likely, you know it all too well. Bad kind of karma is the type that allows you to steal a car that falls apart in front of a police station. Life is good. Bad karma can be such a good friend. it is there for you in good times and bad. It reminds you daily how close it is.

Life is constantly kicking me in the teeth. Usually, it does this right after kicks me down the stairs. It makes me feel so special to wake up in the morning and realize my dignity and pride is about to receive a moderately painful castration. You should not be so surprised. Anyone who works for a living knows how unpleasant it is to have to wake up in the mourning. Wait! Did I mean to say something different? I don't think so. As you can probably speculate by the tone, the original idea was to write something light hearted and humorous. As you can definitely tell, I am neither funny nor smart enough to pull off that feat. Instead, you stuck with this mindless dribble. From the time I was born, I wanted to be a talented comedic writer. Three decades later, I can now see that I have made great achievements at being an untalented hack. It is not my fault. Life is not funny. The wonderfulness that existence has become makes it impossible to find the humor. Life keeps getting in the way of laughter. It is like following a horse carriage on the expressway.

I know it is not just my life that has turned into this recurring nightmare. The vast majority of us wake up in the morning to go to a dead end job. We bust our [backs] for barely enough money to buy gas for the car. Thus, by the end of the month, we can no longer afford to get back to our second homes. We all do this just so we can wake up and find out that we have been out sourced to a foreign planet. Great! Now, we can pay the "Another Being Is Doing Your Job Tax," or the "Foreclosure of The Future Tax." The good news is, you do get a choice of which one you pay. The bad news is that both taxes are 94 per cent of what you have left. The nightmare continues morning after painful mourning. Don't worry! There is an upside to the direction that life is heading.

More and more people are jumping on bandwagons. Lobbying and political correctness has enthralled so many people. Everyone is so busy worrying about what we say or do that no one has time to worry about the fact that there are not enough recycled food stamps to buy a bread crumb for the family. While we are enjoying the inability to speak our minds, or drive and smoke at the same time, we can all wither down to the size of the ever so sexy super models that share a leaf of lettuce for lunch. We are all being force fed ideal, instead of being allowed to work for grocery money. Now that we are all unemployed and can no longer afford food, we might as well have something new on our plates besides the stale taste of another company closing its doors. It is just a good thing that we are all full on their force fed stupidity.

The Lobotomy Experiment

I have done a lot of great things to destroy any chance to brag about my life. Instead of becoming a writer at a young age, I decided to wait until I had time and money. In retrospect I probably should not have done that. I probably should have stayed focused. Over the course of my life, I have always found living for the present easier and more important than gazing out and focusing into a future which is now as desolate and pointless as a warm glass of sewer water. Okay, maybe this not the most appetizing of sediments. Did I mean sentiments? Again, I remind you life stole my humor. I guess I really didn't need to remind anyone.

Life is funny. I remember a friend once asked me to come and work with him. It was a pay cut, so I promptly turned it down. He now lives in a million dollar estate with his beautiful family. I, on the other hand, owe back rent to my x-girlfriend, for that studio apartment we shared with her sister. Sorry, I again find myself strolling down the wrong path. This time it is my mind that went astray in oppose to my decision making skills.

Somehow, I mange to stumble upon a fork in the road, more often than one might expect. I find myself staring blankly ahead and deciding the path to a happy present is much more inviting, than a dimly lit path to a secure future. It never seems practical to venture down a road that starts out with a sacrifice. The road that starts out with an instant reward and then fades into the darkness always seemed more logical than a path that starts out miserably then instantly turns dark. As I grew to realize, the lobotomy experience always leads to choosing the wrong path. It forces you to look back and change your decisions after the fact. Most people experience the same obstacles. As with most rules, there are some exclusions. Incidentally, I have not spoken to my friend since he got that promotion. The vast majority of us are not that fortunate.

Throughout life, everyone is faced with a series of forks in the road. Each path leads us into an elaborate labyrinth. It is here we find ourselves carefully picking and choosing our directions. Every time we choose correctly, we are rewarded. Every time we follow the wrong path, we find our selves deeper in the maze. Sadly, life does not come equipped with road maps. No one chooses our path for us. We make our own decisions.

The more we choose correctly, the better the life we will have. However, we can all take some solace in the knowledge that no matter which path we choose, we can find our way out of the maze. We can change our paths. Well, I guess it would be more accurate to state that we are never doomed after we lead our selves astray. Each fork in the road leads us into another maze. Of course, in the rare event you choose the right direction, the lighted path of a slightly better than mediocre existence can actually become visible.

Sure, it is easy to argue. It is also easy to argue that people's lives are mapped out eons before they are ever born. This mentality is the perfect crutch. No real drive ever needs to be made. We can collectively sit back, enjoy a beer, and blame a predetermined, faulty, and imaginary GPS. Nothing beats kicking off your shoes, and relaxing to the thought that a miserable life is the only way. The faulty GPS is to blame as you sit there, walking down a narrow and narrow minded path.

I found it easy to continue down that same tight fitting hole of a road for decades. I am sure I do not need to tell anyone what a pain in the…neck…it was to find a new path. I became enthralled in the melancholy repetition of blaming the world for my own my mistakes. By time I opened my eyes, it was almost too late to correct a lifetime of short comings. Life was just so much more tolerable when it was not my fault. I was just a victim. I was a prisoner of destiny.

Though a prisoner of destiny may sound like a cheesy love ballad from twenty years ago, it was the ball and chain that kept me happily blaming everyone else for my own mistakes. It was the next step in the experiment of brain dead choices. It left me unable to think clearly. No one thinks clearly. We are all subjects in life's little sociology experiment. Life set up the lobotomy experiment. It has trapped us like mice. It is kind of funny how we carry on in life's elaborate ruse.

Continuously, we enter the path, continue into the maze, and smile as one of the roads we had taken was the right one. Mediocre seems closer than usual. Life can start being humorous again. I, on the other hand… am still not funny. Sadly I am still not bright enough to be a comedic. Perhaps, I have yet to find the correct path. The entire point to life is to find your own way. The only way to achieve happiness is to make sacrifices and blindly stagger into a more tolerable future.

The present only presents the gift of happiness now. Tomorrow, happiness will be in the past and the future will still look dark. All we can do is find the right paths, exit the labyrinths of misguided decisions, and enjoy the present of a happy future.

Through Jeff's Eyes

I woke up one morning, gnawing at my own flesh. It was a habit I had for years. There was nothing more invigorating than the salty metallic taste of my own cud. For me, nothing was better than the taste of blood to wake up in the morning. It was the equivalent to putting extra sugar in a strong coffee. It was the full flavored richness that more people should have learned to enjoy.

It amazed me how many people remained searching for something more fulfilling out of life, but would not embrace the taste of human flesh. They were all so quick to judge, as if they were so perfect. Because of them, I was forced to keep locked inside myself. If only they had known how they made me feel. Again, I was forced to remind myself that they would not understand.

Each and every morning, I would wake up with an insatiable hunger. The novelty of my own version of a morning cup of coffee was wearing thin. The salty metallic taste only lasted while the thick richness was still fresh in my mouth. The sounds of people walking past my window would instantly rinse away the taste.

Every time I would hear them, I would know that it was only a matter of time before I would need something stronger. Quickly, I walked to the window. I needed to see them cry. I needed them to feel as empty as I did. Every laugh brought me closer to acting on my repressed dreams.

I tried to think of the day my dreams first began. No matter what I did, I became too hungry to think. It pained me to continue. I detested myself for who I had become. I hated them for making me who I was. If only they knew they were to blame for my dreams as well as my hunger, then maybe they would not be so quick to judge me. Each laugh that I had heard made it harder to separate myself from my dream.

I could not remember how they began. I guessed it would have been more accurate to state that I did not care to remember. I was young. I could recall feeling something very strange. My mind would drift and I would be asleep. I could see myself standing in a forest on the edge of a violent stream.

There was a man drowning. He was waving for me to help him, but I would stand there just watching. I was overcome with anticipation and I could feel myself smiling. As he fell under the water, I jumped in to save him. He was not conscience when I swam him back to shore.

I stared at him for a moment and realized how hungry I had become. I knelt down, stabbing him the chest. Within a few moments, I had sliced him into thousands of bite sized pieces. Every last mouth watering bit was better than the one I had eaten before it. All that remained was a pile of bones. I threw them back into the water and sat down. At last, I was free to enjoy the silence.

This dream recurred more often as the years past. I found it harder to separate my hunger from how much I detested people. I knew I would have to end their laughter and control my hunger. With both the novelty of my morning feast and my patience of their smiles wearing thin, I would have to act on my hunger. The world would thirst for my name. I would have my revenge. I would feast on the knowledge that I would live on in the memory of the world.

As the time of day began to rise, so did my hunger for revenge. I cleaned my apartment and showered. I spent the morning setting everything in its proper place. I had to make my home perfect. I had to ensure my guest would feel comfortable. I felt butterflies dancing in my stomach. My nerves were still rising as I left the small, tidy home.

I needed to go shopping. The dull blades of the kitchen knives would not do. They needed to be new. They needed to be sharp and flawless. I needed to be sharp and flawless. I thought about how to satisfy my ambitions. I needed to justify my resentment for humanity. I needed a bottle of wine. The butterflies' dance was making it increasingly difficult to concentrate. Focus was a must if I was to succeed at destroying these parasitic maggots.

I felt myself getting ahead of my thought process. I had to stay in control. Nothing and no one could deter me. Concentration and that set of knives would ensure success. My hands were shaking so much. The butterflies must have flown into my arms. My mind hurt as I began over thinking. Suddenly, I felt so empty and cold. Everyone around me was laughing. I hated them.

I wanted to make my way back home, but something stopped me. I was overwhelmed by a salty metallic taste. Usually, the flavor over took me in the morning. Focusing on the hunger was making it hard not to bite my lip. I looked around. No one can look in my direction. I try to speak but they would quickly turn away. Constantly, the world neglected me. Constantly, they would make me who I was. Perhaps, I was too ugly for them to look at me. Perhaps, they knew how ugly they made my mind. I wanted something for them. If they could only see the condescending look on their faces, than they would understand why I hated to see them smile. They were to blame for making me that hungry. They smiled and conversed so openly with each other. Each time I would attempt to make peace, they would turn away. Why? What had I done to deserve that treatment? I did not expect an answer. I just needed to find a piece of mind.

I set my eyes on someone. He was all too content walking alone. It did not seem to bother him that the world was quick to turn its back. His eyes had to be opened. There was no reason to accept neglect. Nobody should settle for second rate treatment. No one should have the right to feel above someone. They made us inferior. As a result, they would be treated equally.

I followed the young man out of the store. He was too naive. He was so easy to follow. It was imperative to get his routine. I stalked his every movement for a few days. My home was clean and ready for him. My thoughts were not. There was no room for error. I could leave nothing to chance.

Anything out of place would bring failure. It was what they expected of me. I would prove to them wrong. It was the logical choice. They have made me suffer through out my life. They caused my recurring dream and my hunger. Once everything was perfect, I reacted on my ambitions.

I had stalked my prey for a few days more. He led me to a neighborhood bar. I waited a few minutes and then entered. I could not be too eager. Seeming too desperate would have ended my revenge prematurely. I waited at the door watching him for awhile. He seemed to be alone and happy. No one gave him a second look. He appeared fine sitting there watching the world move around him.

Not a person in the small hell hole was even willing to glance in his direction. He was dirt. He was nothing more than a void in available seating. I walked over and sat down next to him. Quietly, I ordered a drink. My hunger returned. The caterpillars of nerves had hatched from their cocoons and the newly formed butterflies began to dance.

Sipping my drink, I contemplated how to control my hunger. It became necessary to open this young man's eyes. I looked over and introduced myself. To my surprise, his demeanor did not change. He had become so placid. He was willing to be a fly on the wall of life. I realized that it was my responsibility to free him.

Again, I made an effort to start a conversation. Reluctantly, he responded with a suspicious expression. It was obvious that he was in denial that he deserved more out of life. However, I stayed focused. His ignorance was my focal point. He gradually became comfortable opening up to me.

The bar closed and I knew it was time to free him from himself. He was smiling and laughing. He wanted more to drink and I wanted to save him. It took some time, but I convinced him to join me for a night cap.

The wine was chilled. There is nothing better than a chilled Merlot. The color alone would wake me up. Shortly after entering, I had the cork scraping against the glass bottle. The cork screw was brand new and still had a nice sharp point. It went in so easily that my new friend never even moved as I shoved it into the back of his head.

Instantly, he collapsed into the table. I took the knife from the new set. I blacked out. All I could see was the dream. By time I opened my eyes, I had him sliced into several parts. It was not the thousands of bite size pieces that I had hoped for, but it was a start. The apartment was covered in blood and flesh. The savory flavor was more invigorating than I expected. I felt full for the first time.

It took all night and most of the afternoon to clean my apartment. Blood and entrails were almost impossible to remove from the wood floor. I studied every detail of the night. While examining my actions, from the time I found someone to save to the time I finished scrubbing the apartment, I saw room for improvements.

I spent my free time rethinking my actions. There were too many flaws. I worked too hard to truly enjoy my victory. At the same time, my hatred for humanity began to consume me. I could not separate my thoughts from my hunger. The world turned its back on me. It ignored me. I refused to give in to the silence. I needed them to know who I was.

I could not bring myself to let anyone else look away from me. Never again would anyone find it easy to shut me out of their life. I knew that I needed to make them suffer. They destroyed my confidence early in life. They needed to feel just as empty as I felt. My loathing led to hunger.

I began stalking new victories. The first of which was another young man who was a content loner. He was content enough that he turned his back on me in the middle of a sentence. I forced him to open up to me. I could not be deterred. In time, my persistence was rewarded. He grew to accept me.

When he was finally comfortable, I had him over for dinner. We shared insights about life while enjoying a glass of Merlot. I just could not come to grips with his constant laughing. The smirk was constantly there. He had such judgmental eyes. I had no choice. I shoved them both back out of the sockets. He put more of a struggle than his predecessor. I had to thrust a knife into him, repeatedly. There was too much blood. I had not planned well enough. His screams were too loud. I spent all night and well into the afternoon cleaning. I had to rethink my actions. I knew I could do a much better job.

I still had a full freezer full of food. Knowing this gave me the time to prepare the apartment. It took a few months to reset my focus. During this time, I met a friend. He was empty and alone. He was happy. I wanted to open his mind to the world around him. I needed him to realize that he was just a pawn for the world to silence. He would not bring himself to trust me. Everyone ignored him for so long that he ignored the problem. He could not open his mind to fact that he had right to be heard. He had a right to be understood. Humanity closed his mind. I had no choice, but to open it.

I set down a plastic table cloth. I scrubbed the apartment and then went to the store. I was out of wine and knew I would need a bottle. With the new Merlot on ice and the apartment spotless, I was ready to open my friends mind. I invited him for dinner.

Without hesitation, he accepted. He came over and had dinner. We talked and he was constantly laughing and smiling. He was still blind. He still refused to open his mind. I had no other choice. I stood behind him, listening to him laugh. Placing the knife to his throat, I waited for my opportunity.

As he began to laugh again, I could feel each little groove of the knife scraping against his throat. He was in shock. He flapped around for longer than I expected, but the plastic sheets that I hid under the table cloth and throw rug held well. Clean up was easy. By morning, I was waking up gnawing at my flesh.

I felt refreshed. I felt alive. The salty metallic taste was more invigorating than it had had it been in years. That morning, I woke up hungry. It was not the usual hunger. It was not the normal disdain I had felt for years. I reached into the freezer and helped myself to my first friend.

While I eating my breakfast, I realized that I lost sight of my goal. I had set out to have the world thirst for the knowledge of who I am. I needed to make new friends. I needed to save more people. The noises from outside reminded me that I needed to remain focused. I knew I had no alternatives

The following day, I bought a new a freezer. I reset my apartment contemplating new dishes to satisfy my hunger. My mind hurt. I needed to set my eyes on someone who had to be saved. Laughter and smiles everywhere I looked only fueled my suffering. It was so easy for them. They could laugh and smile at each other. They could talk to each other as if I was never there. On seldom occasions, I would try to initiate conversation. Every time they could only look into my eyes for a few seconds. All of them would look for an escape. They needed to seek out someone else. They wanted to prove they were superior to me. They were better than me. I detested them for it.

I hated them. I hated myself. I was hungry again. I went to the store and for my supplies. I would need plenty of wine. They needed to suffer. They needed to be saved. I bought enough necessities to save many of the content, miserable lives that hide inside themselves as the world moved to isolate them.

I was able to save more without any problems. I felt no remorse for the lives I saved. As the months past, I had saved ten more people. Each friend I saved was easier then the one before. I saved fifteen people from the suffering. During the months that past, my work had finally been noticed. My friends' names were still not in the news. I noticed I still hungered for more. It would not have been enough to have them recognized. I craved that recognition. It was mine. I had earned that respect. For some reason, they still refused to even question who I was. I needed to answer it, even if they refused to ask.

I made a new friend. We remained friends for some time. I thought about the fact that I would have save him. I knew he would turn on me. I knew he would smile. He would eventually laugh and force my hands around his throat.

I clenched so tightly that his head came free from his shoulders. There was nothing left of his neck, but the skin stuck to my hands. I closed his eyes and sliced him into thousands of bite sized pieces. By this time, I had the freezer padlocked to keep my secret safe until the time was right. It took some time to clean up. I was tired and weak. I was ashamed of myself.

I had let my emotions control my actions. Until then, I allowed my motivation to save people be my guide. I knew that I would only be remembered if I remained careful. The thirst for my name and my gifts to the world could only happen if I controlled my emotions. I drank with a few friends and admittedly drugged others. The ones that I drugged was not my fault. The never understood what I trying to do for them. I knew I had to change my focus. As I did, I regained trust that I was making a difference.

I began to read the paper while I was at work. Not one of my friends was ever mentioned. Not one was ever missed. They had been missing for months, yet no one noticed. In death, they were just as invisible as they were in life. I needed their names made public. I had no choice I needed to free them from themselves. This thought forced my hunger to rise. Flashes of blood and torture passed in front of my eyes. The vivid images of the mutilation consumed my every thought. I began biting my lip and the insides of my cheeks. I was in a daze. The salty metallic taste coated my taste buds. I was refreshed and alive. I had never tasted so much of my own blood before that moment.

After work, I bought fresh bottle of Merlot and a new set of knives. I had already finished the last of the wine and knew I would need a bottle or two more. The knives have grown dull. Most of the tips were broken while hacking at bone. After getting home I realized I had forgotten to buy more plastic liners. I could no longer wash the few I had been using. They were too stained and reminded me of my failures. I needed them to be fresh and untainted for my new friend.

We had met a few weeks prior. He was someone I could talk to. He was quiet and had a perpetual frown frozen on his face. I was shocked that he had a natural inability to laugh. We shared stories and drinks with each other. On occasion we would pop pills and proclaim our disdain for society and how arrogant they all were. It was perfect. It remained perfect until I introduced him to someone I had met at the bar I usually frequented. He intrigued me. It was the perfect friendship until I introduced the two. Just as suddenly as the friendships began, they ceased. In an instant I was pushed away and shunned by both. Neither one could look in my direction. Because of them, I went shopping.

I invited one over. I set the liners. While I set the apartment, my mind wandered. The hatred consumed me. Never in my life had I felt such a bitter betrayal. The betrayal was personal. Again, I felt control slipping from my grasps. My dreams replayed in my mind more vividly than I ever seen. I knew I had no choice. I needed to stay focused and in control. Both of my new friends were destined to feel my pain.

When he got to my place, he couldn't even look me in the eyes. He tried so hard to hide his shame. He knew he had betrayed me. I poured the wine and hid my hatred. He did not know I was going to take the carving knife and thrust it repeatedly into his chest. The new knife had no resistance as it filleted him. He did not have a chance to scream. His dead body was still bleeding as it collapsed on to the throw rug. I reached under the Persian rug, grabbed the liner, and dragged the body to the tub. The knives were already in place. I stabbed him and chopped him. I sliced him and blood sprayed everywhere. I took my time. By time I came to and my eyes had opened, his body and blood covered the entire bathroom

A week later, my apartment was still covered in blood. The betrayal had left me with only trace amounts of motivation. I was trapped in a daze. I was lost inside myself and became unable to dictate my own actions. Quietly, I went through the motions of life. I knew nothing of what I was saying and never comprehended what I was doing.

As the weeks turned into months, I was trapped inside the betrayal. The salty metallic taste had lost its vigor. I was an empty shell walking through life unaffected by others. The thought that people would thirst for my name, abandoned me as life had so many years ago.

The next thing I remembered was seeing my apartment surrounded by unfamiliar people. Cars lined the streets and flashes of lights burned my eyes. There was so much chaos and panic. I could not take it any more than I could handle seeing my freezer outside the apartment. Everyone was pointing and yelling at me. I could not understand why.

For the first time since I was a boy, people took notice to me. They hated me for setting the fifteen young men free. They came running over to me and threw me to the ground. My head was bleeding as they cold steel clamped around my wrists. It seemed instantly upon my arrival that I was taken into custody. Not even a breath later I was being accused of setting free the lives of two more than I remembered. I tried to recall who they were. It must have happened while I was still in a daze. It bothered me. I was not offended from being accused. I was bothered that I could not enjoy the beauty of slicing open the two others. I would have wanted to know how they died. I would have wanted to know how much they suffered.

Even after my trial, I was still unsure how I had gone about freeing them. I was consumed by the thoughts of what led me to this solitary confinement. I was blinded by the thought. I could not see that I had accomplished my life's work. From the time of my arrest, the world knew my name. For all of eternity, no one would forget me. While they spent their time thirsting for knowledge of who I was, I was able to say good bye.

Life had begun to come back to light. I was finally able to see life as it truly was. My eyes were open to reality. I was able to see clearly for the time in almost a year. For over two decades no one knew my name or cared and stayed away from even looking at me. Life was perfect and yet I was still shocked when suddenly I keeled over. My head was throbbing and all could see was a large man standing over me and on me. Within minutes of being beaten, I was walking towards this light. My life was over, but my memory will live on forever.

www.ingramcontent.com/pod-product-compliance
Lightning Source LLC
LaVergne TN
LVHW102036110826
845152LV00023B/133/J

* 9 7 8 0 5 7 8 0 0 8 2 6 4 *